Maybe Life's Just *Not* That Into You

When You Feel Like the World's **Voted You OFF**

HOWARD BOOKS
A DIVISION OF SIMON & SCHUSTER
New York   London   Toronto   Sydney

Martha Bolton • Brad Dickson

Comedy Writers for Bob Hope and Jay Leno

Howard Books, a division of Simon & Schuster, Inc.
1230 Avenue of the Americas, New York, NY 10020
www.howardpublishing.com

Maybe Life's Just Not That into You © 2007 Martha Bolton and Brad Dickson

Library of Congress Cataloging-in-Publication Data

Bolton, Martha, 1951-
    Maybe life's just not that into you : when you feel like the world's voted you off / Martha Bolton and Brad Dickson
        p. cm.
    Includes bibliographical references.
    10 Digit ISBN: 1-58229-659-6; 13 Digit ISBN: 978-1-58229-659-3
    1. Life—Humor. 2. Self-help techniques—Humor. 3. Behrendt, Greg—Parodies, imitations, etc. I. Dickson, Brad. II. Title.

PN6231.L48B65 2007
813'.54—dc22
                                                                2006049677

10 9 8 7 6 5 4 3 2 1

HOWARD colophon is a registered trademark of Simon & Schuster, Inc.

Manufactured in the United States of America

For information regarding special discounts for bulk purchases, please contact Simon & Schuster Special Sales at 1-800-456-6798 or business@simonandschuster.com.

Edited by Between the Lines
Cover design by John Lucus
Interior design and parody book covers by John Mark Luke Designs
Photography by Chrys Howard
Illustrations by Dennis Hill

We dedicate this book to our friends
and loved ones and to all the self-help authors
whose positive thinking, hot-coal walking,
mantra chanting, and exclamation-point using
made writing this book easy and fun.

Contents

Acknowledgments

We would like to thank:

Denny Boultinghouse who caught the vision of this book;

Philis Boultinghouse for her patience, encouragement, and her sense of humor;

Our editor **Dawn Brandon** of Between the Lines for keeping us on track;

Ts'ai Lun, Chinese inventor, who invented paper;

And to **all of you** who have ever felt like the world has voted you off, may you find solace within the pages of this book.

Welcome to the Wonderful World of Self-Help . . . or Not

Anyone who's visited a bookstore lately has surely noticed that the shelves are jam-packed with self-help books. On the surface this would make you think people are eager to make the best of themselves. That they want to improve on their health, their attitudes, and relationships, no matter how many steps it takes. That they want to lose their bad habits and excess weight, make better financial decisions, make more and better friends, and age gracefully. The fact that you've picked up this particular self-help book, however, can only mean one thing: you've tried all those other books, and you're still a mess.

Well, maybe it's time to face some cold, hard facts. Some people in life seem to have been blessed with the Midas touch— everything they put their money, energy, and talent into turns to gold. And then there are those who have more of a monsoon touch. Everything they put their money, energy, and talent into turns to mud and slides down a ravine, taking everything in its path with it. Does that sound like you? If it does, don't despair. You are not alone. There are plenty of others just like you out there . . . like that guy standing behind you on the bus, reading this book over your shoulder right now—he's feeling your pain. Or the woman sitting next to you on the flight to Atlanta (everyone goes through Atlanta) pretending to read the safety instructions but all the while looking sideways to read every word you're reading at this exact moment. Don't believe us? Put your finger right here, right over these words, right now, then turn in their direction. See, they got embarrassed, didn't they?

But forget about them. Let's get back to you. If they want to improve themselves, let them buy their own book.

Before we begin improving you, however, we'll need to forewarn you that this book won't make you a millionaire, improve your relationships, or even help you make better first impressions. What it will do is help you come to terms with your lot in life. Maybe you're just not in the same league as Donald Trump, Bill Gates, and Steve Jobs. And let's face it, reading a wide-spaced book with large print isn't going to turn you into those people—or give you their same bank account balance. But it's not your fault. The simple fact may be that life just isn't that into you.

Once you realize this, you can stop beating yourself up. So what if you've made poor financial choices in the past. That's the past. This book will help you focus on the future. Chances are your future choices won't be any wiser, but after reading this book, you just might feel a little better about those 24-percent-interest credit cards and watching your car get repossessed. It's all about attitude. It's about the fine art of whining. It's about losing your shirt but keeping your dignity. It's about being dull and boring but making it work for you. It's about getting in shape, but only so you can beat everyone else to the front of the buffet line. It's about losing friends and influencing nobody and about just saying no to dieting because, well, let's be honest—carbs taste good!

In this unique book, we have borrowed wisdom from some of the best and most popular self-help books on the market and have put our own unique spin on them. How much real wisdom remains is debatable, but hopefully, we've included more laughs than many of these books. And, after all, laughter is the best self-help of all—for winners and losers alike.

This book is for a unique audience. It's not for people who have been dealt only one or two raw deals. It's for people who've had all of life delivered on the rare side. It's for those who've bought stock the night before the market crashed—or discovered too late that their new house is not only sitting on an earthquake fault, it's also in the shadow of a dormant volcano that suddenly started spewing hot lava when they signed on the dotted line. It's for people who can't seem to win no matter how hard they try. It's for those who love life but somehow seem to have really ticked it off.

Maybe Relationships
Just Aren't That
Into You

Chapter 1

The Rules: How to Stay Single into Your Eighties

Unfortunately, in this day and age young people are rushing into marriage far too quickly. It's commonplace for a man and woman of only forty or fifty years of age to decide they want to spend the rest of their lives together and take that life-changing walk down the aisle! We understand the desire to leap into matrimony, yet we can't escape the nagging feeling that some people may be taking this plunge at such an early age because they don't know there's an alternative.

There is! There really, really is!! (Excuse the overuse of exclamation points, but to qualify for self-help book status, there's an exclamation-point quota that must be reached.) Today, thanks to our self-help from self-help books, you can learn how to stay single well into your eighties—and beyond!

Here are some tips:

1. A young woman should maintain a certain "hard to get" aura. This can be accomplished in a number of ways. For example, if you're walking down the street and a man says

hello to you, look the other way immediately, and run back to your apartment. Screaming, "Quit looking at me, scumbag!" also helps guarantee your singleness for years to come.

2. If a potential date somehow manages to acquire your phone number (say he or she gets it from one of your friends or reads it off of your check while standing in line at the grocery store), never ever answer the telephone when this person calls. Especially on the weekend. Answering the phone on the weekend is a major faux pas. It lets the person know that you're just sitting at home and have no life. You may very well be sitting at home and have no life, but why telegraph that to others?

    If, however, the person calls during the week, you may answer the phone—but never before the twenty-fifth ring. Waiting this long will make the caller think you're busy, even if you're just sitting there trimming your chin hairs and counting the telephone rings.

    If the ringing continues beyond the twenty-fifth ring, feel free to answer the phone. But do not, we repeat, do not use your regular voice. Use your "sick" voice, and tell the person you have to take medicine to control a highly contagious strain of monkeypox you contracted at the flea market. (You may want to actually get monkeypox so you're not purposely misleading anyone.)

    Be forewarned, however, that for women this plan can backfire. Historically, men want what they can't have, and a quarantine is just such a lure. But hang tough. In some instances, telling a potential suitor that you have a near-fatal disease might prove safer than actually conversing and falling into the trap of agreeing to a date. Before your eighteenth birthday, that is.

3. If a man meets all the standard qualifications for dating (he has a Blue Blood family lineage, is over 6' and under 6' 2", is named Trevor, Barkley, or William VII, and has obtained an Ivy League degree or an Olympic medal or has climbed Mt. Everest in under six days), then a woman may agree to go on a single date with the suitor. But she should arrive at the restaurant in a separate car and never make eye contact with the man during the meal. Eye contact is deadly on a date. Avoid eye contact at all costs, and only engage in superficial conversation, such as, "I'll have the steak and lobster, please."

4. On a dinner date, it's important for a woman to take no more than four bites of the steak and lobster dinner she orders. This will let her man know that she is more than happy to waste his money. Men love this. She should let the waiter take away the barely touched $29 entree while she explains to her date that she "can't eat another bite," and then she should order the $7 Bananas Foster.

    The most important dinner-date rule for a man to remember is to forget to bring his wallet.

5. Another important rule to remember—in fact the most important rule for staying single into your eighties—is no hand-holding, hugging, or kissing (even on the cheek) before the forty-fourth date. In fact, we recommend that the person not driving sit in the rear seat.

6. Women should never, ever, ever call a man. We realize that in today's society, many women do this. But it's not wise or proper behavior for a woman seeking to maintain her singlehood into her eighties. If you are in need of emergency aid and dial 911 and a man answers, HANG UP IMMEDIATELY. It's just not worth the risk. And women should never ask a man out. It is a man's lot in life to risk the humiliation and disappointment of asking a woman out. If you do the asking, you deny him this ego-bursting opportunity.

7. Men should never show their vulnerable side to a woman. No matter how many times you watch that replay of your favorite team losing the Super Bowl, do not cry. Save this display of emotion for your buddies who will understand.

8. Men, if you spot a woman you consider attractive, whatever you do, don't tell her you think she's good-looking. Instead, say that you find her to be revolting. That way you'll throw her into a self-esteem crisis, and she'll be in therapy for years. This will also keep anyone else from wanting the woman, making sure she stays available while you remain free to enjoy your singlehood. This rule also applies to women.

9. If a man tries to take your hand (even if it's to help you up after you've slipped in a rain puddle), pull it back and shout, "Get back! I've just been diagnosed with that dreaded, highly contagious flesh-eating virus. What's the matter with you?"

10. If a woman suggests taking you home to meet her mother, this is akin to walking the plank. Usually there's no return, so think long and hard about accepting this invitation, no matter how good her mama's cooking is.

Do the above, and we can almost guarantee you'll reach your eightieth birthday without having to pick up a single dirty sock of Prince Charming's or lose one minute's sleep to his snoring.

Factoid
Some self-help authors are educated at the finest barber colleges.

Men Are from Neptune,
Women Are from Saturn

To understand how couples can make their relationship work, it's important first to realize that men and women are as inherently different as night and day, as unlike as fire and ice, as diverse as milk and soda, as distinct as the desert and the sea, as incompatible as a turtle and a hare, as opposite as love and hate, as contrary as Bill O'Reilly and Jesse Jackson. In other words, men are from Neptune, women are from Saturn.

When faced with choices, Neptunians (men) react one way, and Saturnians (women) react in an entirely different manner. For example, say it's a hot day and the Saturnian wants the Neptunian to mow the yard. But because the nighttime temperature on Neptune is something like minus 220 degrees Celsius, Neptunians are not used to even being outdoors—so of course the Neptunian refuses. The Saturnian does not understand this refusal. She feels it's nice enough to perform outdoor activities. And she finally convinces the Neptunian that it is indeed safe enough to go outside, but instead of mowing the lawn, he opts for golf instead. The Saturnian isn't happy, and that, as all scientists know, is what really caused the original Big Bang. It had nothing to do with the beginning of the world. God created the heavens and the earth. The Big Bang, or Big Explosion, was all about a man, a woman, and golf.

Need more convincing? Here's another example. Say the Saturnian wants the Neptunian to help with the dishes rather than to go watch the big game on his new plasma TV with his buddies. Now, as he is from the planet farthest from the sun, the Neptunian has always had some abandonment issues, so he naturally feels excessively deprived by not being allowed to join his friends.

You might think the Neptunian would sink into a deep depression over missing the game with his buddies, but he knows enough to pinpoint the real problem: it lies in their inherent differences. Men are from Neptune; women are from Saturn. The wise Neptunian knows that as long as he's going to live in this galaxy, there's no getting around this fact of life. Some differences between a man and a woman just have to be adapted to.

Say the Neptunian would like the Saturnian to have dinner ready when he comes home from working hard. But the Saturnian has worked hard, too, and doesn't see why she has to cook dinner. So they opt to go out to eat. But since they are from different planets, they can't agree on where to eat. So they argue while driving around town, and since they're hungry, the argument escalates into interplanetary warfare.

It doesn't have to be like this. If only Neptunians and Saturnians would learn to meet somewhere in neutral territory—say, Jupiter—to resolve these differences, the entire universe could be a happier place. But leave Mars alone. According to a recent study, there are already too many self-help authors living there.

What All Women Need the Men in Their Lives (Who Are Generally Clueless) to Know

- I need you to know that I need frequent reassuring that our relationship is vital and important to you.

- I need you to know that I enjoy your simply holding me and being with me.

- I need you to know that I like to be told that you love me and that you want to be with me.

- I need you to know that I want to be the most important thing in your life, but not the only thing in your life.

- I need you to know that I love it when you surprise me, whether it's with flowers, candy, or just that brief little e-mail that says, "Hi, there—I'm thinking of you."

BONUS SECTION:
What Men Need Women to Know about Them

- I like the TV remote left on the coffee table.

The Relationship Pop Quiz

Too many people enter marriage without a clue as to who their partner really is. They wake up one morning and realize they've been married to a total stranger for five, ten, maybe even fifty years. Who is that person sitting across the breakfast table, crunching on All-Bran—or standing over the bathroom sink trimming his toenails? Who are these people, and how in the world did they get into our houses?

To help you avoid this type of relationship disaster and to find out exactly how well you know the person you're dating or married to, take the following Relationship Pop Quiz.

1. The guy or girl I'm in love with . . .
   a. is right-handed.
   b. is left-handed.
   c. is ambidextrous.
   d. uses his or her toes to type.

Chapter 1

2. What color hair does he have?
   a. Brown
   b. Blond
   c. Red
   d. He only has a tiny bit of hair on one side of his head, but he combs it over, and he looks ridiculous—like an eel sunbathing on a rock. So to answer your question, his hair would be "eel colored."

3. What is his or her occupation?
   a. Pilot
   b. Physician
   c. Pizza delivery driver
   d. Not sure, but I think it has something to do with sailing, as he or she is always mumbling, "One day my ship will come in."

4. What is the person's usual mode of transportation?
   a. Automobile
   b. Train
   c. Hitchhiking
   d. Scooter

5. She is . . .
   a. tall.
   b. short.
   c. just right.
   d. I never really noticed her height, because I'm usually looking at myself in a mirror.

6. What's his or her favorite food to order at a restaurant?
   a. Steak

    b. Pasta

    c. Vegetarian dish

    d. I can't remember, because the last time we went out to dinner was April 12, 1973.

7. She comes from . . .

    a. a large family.

    b. a small family.

    c. no family. She's a clone.

    d. It depends on whether you count her multipersonalitied mother as one person or eight.

8. His most endearing quality is . . .

    a. his sense of humor.

    b. his remarkable intelligence.

    c. his good looks.

    d. his big fat wallet.

9. Your significant other's hobby is . . .

    a. collecting stamps.

    b. playing tennis.

    c. going to ball games.

    d. Because it takes her five hours to get ready to leave the house, there's no time for a hobby.

10. He or she wears . . .

    a. cutting-edge fashion.

    b. thrift-store apparel.

    c. a jogging suit.

    d. nothing but "I'm with Stupid" T-shirts.

He's Really, Really Just Not That Into You—Not One Bit Whatsoever

Folks, you deserve the best! You deserve to be placed on a pedestal higher than the Empire State Building. If that guy or girl you're dating isn't going to do this, we suggest you move on. Consider the following letter we received just the other day:

Dear Brad and Martha,

I've been with my boyfriend, whom I'll call Jim (which is part of the reason he's mad at me—his real name is Phil, but I keep forgetting). Anyway, we've been dating for almost fourteen years. I've heard you speak before on the benefits of remaining single into your eighties, but Jim has been a good, loyal, and attentive companion. My problem is that last Tuesday, for the first time in our relationship, he forgot the anniversary of the first time we ordered crème brûlée together. He remembers all our other anniversaries—our first date, the first time we held hands, the first time we kissed, the first time we said "I love you." But I would think that the first time we ordered crème brûlée together would be the biggie (it was fabulous crème brûlée), and I'm crushed beyond belief. I feel this was insensitive, hurtful, and rude. I really thought we had something special. What should I do?

Disillusioned in Cleveland

Dear Disillusioned,

Let's make this as simple as possible. Dump the loser! All anniversaries are important, and he might as well learn that now rather than later. Imagine what your life would be like if you were to marry an inconsiderate dead weight like "Jim" or "Phil" or whatever his name is. Girl, you're too bright, too giving, too smart, and too sensitive to put up with this kind of thoughtless treatment. So run, don't walk—just get yourself out of that relationship! And order yourself another crème brûlée to ease your pain.

B. D.

Dear Brad and Martha,

Throughout our long-term marriage, my husband, Paul, is frequently away on Saturday afternoons, either racing automobiles or mixing salad dressing. The rest of the week he's always there for me and very giving. He's never cheated on me, although he's considered by most women to be quite handsome. He's an excellent provider, but he also is supportive of my career goals. How should I deal with this situation?

Joanne Woodward*
Beverly Hills

*Not that Joanne Woodward

19

Chapter 1

Dear Joanne,

This is quite a conundrum, because your husband is generally there for you. However, the fact he's not around on Saturday afternoons and spends this, arguably the most important day of the week, away from the woman he allegedly loves, makes me think you are in dire need of intensive marital counseling. You deserve better than what this self-centered egomaniac is giving you! I suggest you pitch a hissy fit and demand that Paul be there for you every day, including Saturday!

M. B.

Dear Brad and Martha,

My girlfriend answers to the nickname "Pinky." This bothers me.

Moose

Dear Moose,

It should. I once dropped an old boyfriend whose friends called him "Slick." I suggest you consider doing the same with "Pinky." Even if the relationship goes somewhere, people will laugh at the wedding announcement. "Moose marries Pinky"— that sounds like a joke. Is that what you want—a wedding announcement that's a joke? Move on, man, you can do better.

M. B.

Dear Martha and Brad,

I've been married for twelve years and am still madly in love. Every day our relationship seems to grow. I never dreamed I could feel such passion or commitment for another human being. There's only one little problem: a few days ago the love of my life left the toilet seat up. This is the first time he's ever done that. What should I do?

Confused and Hurt in
Cincinnati

Dear Confused in Cincinnati,

If he leaves the toilet seat up, it's obvious he doesn't care for you on a level you deserve. We hate to tell you this, but all indicators point to one simple truth: he's just not that into you. Dry your tears and demand an apology, dinner out, and a new outfit. And if that doesn't make him shape up, tell him your momma's moving in to straighten him out!

M. B.

Dear Brad and Martha,

My girlfriend of seven years has always been a wonderful cook. However, last night she burned the meat loaf. I was planning to ask this woman to marry me, but now I'm reconsidering. What do you think?

Hungry Bill in Buffalo

Dear Hungry,

The key to a guy's heart is through his stomach. The meat loaf she burned never made it to your stomach, thus it's time to cut her out of your heart. On your way out the door, may I suggest a parting gift—a meat thermometer?

B. D.

Men Are Like Driftwood

Many self-help book authors seem to believe firmly in the subordination of the male species.

We're not saying they're wrong.

But we're not saying they're right, either.

Some seem to think that all men are no good. They generalize and liken them to unflattering, even inhuman or inanimate things. You've probably read other self-help books equating men with fish, dogs, cacti, or even pencil sharpeners. These books then go on at great length, advising women how to go about getting one of these pencil sharpeners to marry them.

Then there are self-improvement tomes that parallel men to undesirable things like dust, vinegar, garbage, sea otters, and tissue paper. Gals, if you read enough self-help books, eventually you will have zero respect for men. And therein lies the problem. As a society we have lowered our respect for men and are not treating them with the dignity they deserve.

The authors of this book, however, would never do that.

Rather, we suggest picturing men as driftwood . . . only with a remote control in their hand. Once you picture them this way, you'll find it easier to deal with them.

Driftwood isn't a bad thing. It just floats along, like so much other sea debris. Many men just seem to float along too, waiting for a woman to reel 'em in.

How does a woman reel in driftwood (i.e., a man)? By making herself as appealing to the driftwood as possible. A "driftwood" likes a female who at least pretends to be less intelligent than he is. So never answer a single question on *Jeopardy*.

Catching your own driftwood doesn't require any special knowledge or trade secrets. As with so many things in life, all it takes is a plan.

Plan for Landing Driftwood (i.e., marrying a man)

Just follow these simple steps:

1. Meet driftwood. He's perfect, everything you've ever wanted.

2. Immediately try to change driftwood.

3. After enough successful changes, get driftwood to propose marriage.

4. Marry driftwood.

5. Float in sea happily ever after, just you, your beloved driftwood, and your mother.

Now, was that so hard? Any woman can follow these five simple steps to a lifetime of happiness with the driftwood of her choice! But to be successful, you must always remember to treat your driftwood with the utmost respect. After all, he's not just any driftwood. He's *your* driftwood.

Smart Women Know a Thing or Two

- Smart women know to avoid commitment-phobic men. If they can't commit, you must omit!

- Smart women know that a man who cancels a date at the last minute due to a horrible traffic accident (and the fact that he's in a full body cast in ICU) should be tarred, feathered, and dropped into the wilds of Antarctica to fend for himself. There is absolutely no excuse for canceling a date!

- Smart women know that boyfriends who won't loan you money are a waste of your time and should be treated like gerbils—kept in a cage and forced to run on that little wheel—so at least all the change will fall out of their pockets.

- Smart women know that a man who has other plans on Saturday night is a worm—except he doesn't deserve the consideration you'd give a worm and should simply be stepped on.

- Smart women know a man who refuses to take her to the finest restaurants is probably not going to be a good father either.

- Smart women know that a man who's not a good listener should be given the "van Gogh treatment."

- Smart women know that sometimes they don't know all that much more than smart men.

BONUS SECTION:
Smart Men Know a Thing or Three

- Smart men know that it's best to always agree with a smart woman, even when she's completely wrong.

- Smart men know that to tell your wife her new outfit makes her look hefty is a crime punishable by solitary confinement (which is what the house will feel like after you've made such a remark).

- Smart men know to tell their significant other that they love her cooking even while the stomach-pumping is in progress. Especially while the stomach-pumping is in progress.

Finding Love in All the Not So Great Places

We all want love. Every single one of us. It doesn't matter how much you say you can live without it, the truth is, you can't. Everyone wants to know that he or she means something to someone else. Even if all you've got going for you is that the utilities company sends you a Christmas card, that may be enough to keep you hanging on year after year after year.

But what about true love? Romantic love? Love that's expressed in more meaningful ways than a $480 electric bill? Love that is pure and loyal and unselfish? Love that's real and unending? It's an age-old search, and it can consume us. Where do we even begin to look for this elusive treasure? Ah, yes . . . that, dear reader, is the million-dollar question.

Lucky for you, the answer is right here—within the pages of this book. These pages are dedicated to helping you cut to the chase and find the Holy Grail of modern life: true love. We want you to find it. Not just any love. The love of your life.

You can search high, and you can search low. You can look for love "in all the wrong places," to quote a famous country song.

You can waste your life chasing false love, never having the real thing, or you can study the guide below and conduct your quest for love in a more scientific manner.

Good Places to Search for Love

- singles mixers

- church socials

- dinner parties

- choir practice

- romantic music concerts

- the recommendations of friends

- blind dates (providing the person setting you up is a true friend)

- reputable dating services

- the vegetable aisle at the grocery store

- the Laundromat (but not if it's being robbed and the person taking the quarters out of the machines is the one flirting with you)

Bad Places to Search for Love

- rodeos

- clown conventions

- monthly meetings of the Codependents Therapy Group

- maximum security prison

- any riot

- serial-killer empowerment groups

- pie-eating contests

Even if you initially feel discouraged, don't give up your search for love! Sometimes it can take decades to find the right person for you. So hang in there! And if at some point down the lonely road we call life, you still have not found love, you may want to remove, say, clown conventions and codependent meetings from the lists of places not to search. At this point you will have become what is known as desperate. But that's perfectly OK! After all, many people going on their twentieth, thirtieth, or even fortieth wedding anniversary have been quoted as saying they "married a clown."

Bet You've Heard a Zillion!
THE *MANY, MANY*
LIES
MEN TELL
WOMEN
before Marriage

Lies Men Tell Women

Lies Men Tell Women before Marriage

1. I'm just a little over six feet tall.

2. I drive a brand-new Corvette, and I believe diamonds are a girl's best friend.

3. No, really, about six feet and 1/16 of an inch tall.

4. I make a lot of money.

5. Elevator shoes?! Of course not, why would I wear elevator shoes?

6. I do not enjoy sports and would never waste a beautiful Saturday afternoon doing something as stupid as watching a game on television when I could be shopping at the mall with my sweetie.

7. OK, I'm actually about six feet and 1/32 of an inch tall.

8. I love doing yard work and taking out the garbage.

9. I love you more than the TV remote.

10. OK, you called my bluff. I'm only six feet and 1/187 of an inch tall. In thick socks.

Lies Men Tell Women after Marriage

1. I'll take down the Christmas lights next weekend.

2. I'm fine with missing the Super Bowl so we can go to the craft fair with your mother.

3. I never have any trouble lighting the charcoal briquettes.

4. The most important day of my life? Why, that would be our wedding day. . . . Of course I know when our anniversary is!

5. No, really, I'll take down the Christmas lights next weekend. At the latest, the Fourth of July. I don't have to work that day.

6. Ask directions? Heck, no, I know exactly where I am!

7. I can fix the transmission myself . . . just as soon as I find out what it looks like.

8. You look like you've lost ten pounds.

9. On second thought, make that twenty pounds!

10. Take down the Christmas lights? What for? Christmas is just two months away!

BONUS SECTION:
Lies Women Tell Men

It really isn't all about me.

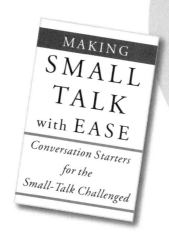

Making Small Talk with Ease

Ever feel like you wanted to approach a stranger but didn't know what to say? All of us are a little shy in certain situations, a little tongue-tied, a little apprehensive. But fear no more! Making Small Talk with Ease will remedy all your conversation reticence! Just whip out this handy pocket guide to find the perfect bon mot for any occasion. Have real icebreakers at your fingertips! Never again be at a loss for words when you see an interesting person you'd like to approach! Network your way to success and power by knowing what to say and when to say it!

Small Talk for Restaurants

- "Excuse me—I thought I saw a fly in your soup . . . Oops, my mistake. That's just a noodle. By the way, my name's Frank."

- "Are you the waitress? No? Well, could you refill my soda anyway? By the way, I'm Frank—and your name is . . . ?"

- "You have nice feet. Are they yours? I'm Frank. And you are . . . ?"

Small Talk for Inclement Weather

- "I like rain—but then again, I own an umbrella. What about you?"

- "I believe we're in the eye of the hurricane. Say, you have nice eyes too. Want to go to Starbucks?"

Small Talk for Airports and Train Stations

- "Statistically, we're in more danger than astronauts flying on the space shuttle. Do you have a living will? By the way, my name's Frank. That's F-R-A . . ."

- "Your shoes look freshly shined. Did you do it yourself or hire one of these shoe-shine experts?"

Small Talk for the DMV

- "I noticed you laughing out loud. I admire anyone who can find mirth while standing in line at the DMV. I only laugh out loud when I'm tickled. Would you like to tickle me?"

- "I'm going to be taking my driving test today. Would you mind standing in my photo with me? By the way, my name is Frank. That's a good color on you."

General Conversation Starters

- "I read a good book the other day. It was called the Dictionary. I now know the meanings of many words. Have you read any good books lately?"

- "I also read the almanac. Did you know the gazelle is the fastest animal, capable of a top speed of eighty-five miles per hour? And that the population of Madrid, Spain, is 2.95 million? The almanac is a fascinating book. I wonder if they'll make a movie out of it."

- "You remind me of my aunt. She has a mustache too. Hi, I'm Frank."

These conversation starters are guaranteed to help you make friends, get dates, and find happiness! With the exception of a few bad eggs who have misinterpreted our tips and now have restraining orders against them, our readers for the most part have been pleased with these conversation starters—and we're reasonably sure that you will be too! Try them. If they work for you, write and tell us. If they don't and you want to write a nasty letter, the name is Frank. That's F-R-A . . .

Can This Rocky Relationship Be Saved?

Dear Brad and Martha,

    My husband is always playing with the kids, working around the house, cooking, dusting, vacuuming, and doing the laundry. He never seems to have time for me! I mention this to him every night at midnight when he comes home from his second job, but he just mumbles something about being exhausted and hands me some roses. Then, just when we start to get—well, you know, all cuddly and everything— he falls asleep and won't stay awake to watch a movie with me! I don't understand this. He doesn't have to be at his first job until six a.m.! I feel he's neglecting me and doesn't care at all about my needs. After sitting around watching my soaps all day and talking on the phone or e-mailing my friends, I'm ready to relax and have some quality time with the man I love. Is our marriage hopelessly dysfunctional?

                         Neglected in Pasadena

Dear Neglected,

Talk about self-absorbed! All you're asking for is one little movie, and he won't even give you that? Sure, you could look at your own behavior and see that maybe you need to change some of your focus and cut him some slack, but what fun is that? We're glad you wrote. You have a right to complain! Plenty of good men work two jobs, are a good father, do all the housework, and still find time to watch a movie with their beloved before drifting off to sleep. True, a good percentage of these good men have already worked themselves into an early grave, but the rest of them are setting a wonderful example for the younger generation. Your marriage isn't hopeless. But he's got to want to change.

Brad and Martha

Dear Brad and Martha,

My wife is constantly harping at me to mow the lawn every weekend. I know I haven't had a job in four years and that she's the breadwinner in the family, but she knows Saturday is my golf day. Do you think this is grounds for divorce?

Unhappy in Milwaukee

Dear Unhappy,

We don't advocate divorce. But we do realize we're talking golf here. Golf. Or let us put it another way—GOLF! Mowing the lawn doesn't even begin to compare with the importance of golf in some men's lives. Your wife may need help realizing this. We suggest taking your wife to a marriage retreat at any of the major golf resorts. If you can find one where Jack Nicklaus or Tiger Woods is the speaker, so much the better. Your marriage is worth it. And do keep us posted on your progress. And your scores.

Brad and Martha

Dear Brad and Martha,

My wife refuses to pick up after herself, and it's really starting to get on my nerves! I'm constantly tripping over her shoes and the piles of clothing she leaves all around the house. Why can't she just put them on the dining-room table, like I do mine? Then she'll always know where they are, and I won't run the risk of breaking my neck every time I try walking through the living room. Am I being petty, or is this grounds for divorce?

Living in a Mine Field,
Kissimmee, Florida

Dear Mine Field,

We're so glad you wrote. You, sir, are certainly living in danger! You could slip and be seriously injured just walking down the hall to get a drink of water. They say marriage is a two-way street, but we prefer thinking of it as a cul-de-sac. In other words, what goes around comes around. Start leaving your clothes and shoes scattered all over the house too. We realize that you're a man, and leaving your things strewn all over the floor is a difficult thing to do, but trust us on this— it'll help your wife see your point. If, however, the piles get so high that they threaten your safety or become snowcapped, it's time to discontinue this exercise and seek counseling.

Brad and Martha

Dear Brad and Martha,

My husband refuses to take the blame for my mistakes. I thought this was one of the elementary items covered in the wedding vows—"Do you promise to love, honor, cherish, and take the blame for both of you as long as you both shall live." He said, "I do." But now he's reneging. The whole reason I married my scapegoat—I mean, husband—in the first place was for this one perk of marriage. And now he's refusing to cooperate! Is there any hope, or should I just leave . . . and blame him for that too?

Blameless in Phoenix

Dear Blameless,

Don't leave, even though not being willing to take the blame for a wife's actions is a fundamental breach of the marital contract. Have the courage to stay tough and hang in there, and hopefully one day you'll have the scapegoat you deserve. Accepting blame for your own behavior is a ridiculous notion. No marriage counselor with a legitimate three-month counseling certificate would endorse this kind of outrageous behavior. We're pulling for you!

Brad and Martha

The Idiot's Handbook to Divorce

In the sad and unfortunate situation where a couple finds themselves heading toward divorce, we feel it's important to give you a heads-up about what to expect before and during this difficult process. And, as with all of our Idiot books (you'll find more later in our comprehensive collection), we will do it in as simple terms as possible.

Stage One: Separation

This is often a bewildering, scary, irritating, agonizing, seemingly freeing, stressful, exhausting, exasperating, poignant, and baffling period when you're suddenly alone for the first time in years. It can be a time of extreme emotions: perceived happiness, hatred, exhilaration, despair, malaise, and all kinds of funky feelings all at once. But hang on! Things will get better.

Stage Two: Anger

This is a normal feeling to experience during and after divorce. For a woman it frequently flares up when, say, running into her ex-husband at the restaurant he always refused to take her to because it was too expensive, only now he's there with his new girlfriend, Bambi or Chloe or some other name better suited to an animal that grazes.

For a man anger may first surface when he realizes his wife not only left him but is fighting for custody of his recliner too! But don't dismay. Anger is a necessary stage in the healing process, so just go with it. Things will get better!

Stage Three: Shock

Shock hits when you realize you're alone in the world with only a battalion of divorce lawyers for comfort and support. Your friends avoid you, and family members who used to pretend they loved you are now venting all their true feelings that had apparently been there all along. But don't sweat it—things will improve soon!

Stage Four: Deep Shock

This is a natural reaction when you find yourself confronting a world that is clearly outside your comfort zone. Hold on—you're almost there! Sure, you have no friends, no money, and maybe even no home, but you're on the road to recovery. You'll be smiling any day now.

Stage Five: Mind-Numbing Shock

This is not a pleasant time, but we promise, you're rounding the corner!

Stage Six: Recovery

Congratulations! It's all downhill from here. It's time to start living your life again and to look forward to a bright future. Sure, you're broke, your self-esteem has gone through the wringer, and your divorce attorney has the best tan he or she has had in years thanks to all the time spent discussing your case on the beach with your ex. But you've made it through. Aren't you so giddy you could almost fly? Go on! Spread your wings and shout, "I'm free as a bird!" Flap those wings, free bird! Fly!

10 Affirmations for the Guilt-Driven

1. I'm sorry. Was my breathing bothering you?

2. You're absolutely right. I'm taking up valuable space on this planet that could go to someone more worthwhile.

3. Everything that has ever gone wrong at any time, past or present, or may go wrong in the future, is entirely my fault. How foolish of me to think otherwise.

4. Let me apologize before I even get to the party.

5. Yes, I am to blame.

6. No, really, I'm to blame.

7. Woe is me. Again.

8. I take full responsibility for the immature actions of all the people in the world.

9. I will apologize 47,385 times today. I'm sorry to bore you with that statistic. (Now I have to make that 47,386 times.)

10. Once again let me repeat: I, and I alone, am to blame. For everything. Everywhere. My fault.

Maybe Finances Just Aren't That Into You

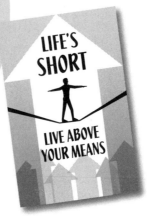

Life's Short: Live above Your Means

Are you going to be one of those financial wimps who lets a mere 24-percent interest rate scare them away from overwhelming credit-card debt? Of course not! You're smart enough to know that credit-card companies wouldn't be sending you all those offers if they didn't think you were good for it. They know a good credit risk when they see one, and even though the offers come addressed to "Occupant" and your two-year-old received the same offer as you (except his application promised a higher credit line and a lower interest rate), that still isn't enough to stop a financial wizard like you from filling out those applications and getting enough credit cards to mosaic your coffee table with the cut-up pieces after the creditors cancel your accounts.

So why wait? Start filling out those applications now, before it's too late and you have to wait a day or so for a new offer to arrive in your mailbox!

Still not convinced? Got cold feet? That's OK—we've all been there. Living above your means is scary at first, but once you get used to it, you'll realize it's a fun way to exist. Why wait for that new boat or Sea-Doo? Buy it today! Why buy that smaller vehicle when you can have the SUV of your dreams? Why sit at home watching the Travel Channel when you can actually be in Paris? Or Rome. Or Zimbabwe! Send today for our free CD (include $129.00 for postage and handling) that will teach you to say, "Charge it!" in fourteen languages.

All your life you've been hearing so-called experts advise, "Live below your means. Pitch a tent on the street corner even if you are a millionaire. Save, save, save! Purchase your parents' fiftieth-anniversary gift at the 99-cent store. Buy used on eBay, even if it's a lifesaving pacemaker you're shopping for. Never buy a pack of chewing gum when you have an endless supply of used gum under restaurant tables and theater chairs the world over."

Nag, nag, nag, nag, nag. All those bean counters take the joy right out of living, don't they?

Granted, it may all be sound advice. But what fun is that?! We're here to tell you there's a better way.

Living above your means can actually be a good thing! No, it's not for the wimpy. Living above your means forces you to rise above your socioeconomic status and reach for the stars . . . or at least higher credit limits.

For example, the authors of this book have a net worth of $873.50 and $1,456.89, respectively. Yet we enjoy the use of fine, imported automobiles, wear top-of-the-line designer clothes, and eat the finest caviar (did you know that means "fish eggs"?). One of us just returned from a beach vacation on St. Tropez. How did we do it? We charged it, of course! Do we have the means to pay it back in our lifetime? Not a dime of it—but hey, no sweat, because the credit-card companies will graciously give us fifty years to pay it off. And if we need more time, we can even defer some of the payments and tack them on at the end. See, we all win. We get to use the items now and only have to pay back thirty times what they're worth!

Now, we know what you're thinking. We're just another author duo trying to get attention for ourselves by going against the grain and saying something outrageous in order to sell our book. To that we say, *"And your point is?"*

We believe life is over before you know it, so why not go out in grand style? We also believe in the adage, "He who dies with the highest unpaid balance on his MasterCard wins." Of course, they could come and repossess the suit you're wearing in your coffin—or for that matter—even the coffin itself; but the point is, what would you care?

So go on, spend like there's no tomorrow. The way the world is going, who knows if there will be a tomorrow. Live it up! If you're an American, you're probably already pretty good at living above your means. So just keep doing what you do best. Spend, spend, spend! If you bought a used copy of this book, go out tomorrow and buy a brand-new one. Buy a bunch of copies and send them to all your friends! Don't allow your credit limit to determine your lifestyle. Go on and charge it and pay that $39 over-the-limit fee and that 24-percent interest to show those credit-card companies who's boss!

Poor Dad, Poorer Dad

It's easy to sort out advice when it's coming from one poor dad and one rich dad. But what if you had two dads, and neither one made good investment choices? What if both were financial losers? Where's the advice book from that perspective? Where's the bestselling book addressing paternal influences from a poor dad, poorer dad perspective?

Where? Why, you're holding it in your hands!

I (name withheld to protect the broke) had two fathers. One lived hand-to-mouth, surviving on food stamps, and was frequently thousands of dollars in debt. And then there was my unemployed dad.

Dad #1 worked two jobs, even putting in overtime, and still he was months behind on his bills.

Dad #2 didn't have much money either, but at least he didn't have to get up in the morning and go to work. He slept in the backseat of a dilapidated 1955 Volvo, and, well, you get the picture.

Because of my two dads and their respective approaches to

all things financial, I have a unique moneymaking ability—like writing a how-to book on finances in order to make my mortgage payment with the advance money. (What I'll do for next month's mortgage payment is yet to be determined.) The point is, I never would have thought of taking such a bold step had it not been for the education my two dads gave me.

What could two financially challenged dads possibly teach me about handling money? Plenty!

Read on and learn.

Years ago, when I was a young person just starting out as an entrepreneur, I went to my poor dad and said, "Dad, I'm thinking of investing in some low-cost apartment houses in New York City. What do you think about that?" And Poor Dad said, "Well, Son, I used to live in a low-cost apartment house, and I can tell you unequivocally, it was a rat trap. The property you're looking at will probably be condemned and have to be torn down, and you'll be left holding a couple of square blocks in downtown Manhattan. What good's that going to do you?"

He had a point, but not wanting to make my decision without input from Poorer Dad too, I went to him and said, "Dad, I'm thinking of investing in some low-cost apartment houses in New York City. What do you think about that?" And he said, "Do it! Sounds like a million-dollar idea. What have you got to lose?"

So I returned home and fed the data from my two dads, or as I called them, Broke and Broker, into the computer I'd made from an old word processor and a toaster. And the computer spit out, "Go with Poor Dad." So I did. I avoided those low-cost apartment houses, and Poor Dad was right. They were later torn down and the site sold to Donald Trump for his Trump Tower, which is all worth a fortune today and . . . OK, poor example.

What I'm trying to say is that by utilizing the advice given me by Poor Dad, who was merely poor, and Poorer Dad, who was a legitimate, card-carrying indigent, I have learned to make financial decisions that have served me well. Not by making me ridiculously wealthy. But by making me perhaps the wisest person in the unemployment line.

The Trump Tower lesson wasn't the only example of how Poor Dad and Poorer Dad helped me in their own unique ways. Years later, when I had an opportunity to invest in Enron stock, I went to Poor Dad and said, "Destitute Daddy, I'm thinking of buying Enron at $77 per share." And he said, "If I were you, I'd just give the money to me instead."

He had a point. But I wasn't going to make my decision without hearing from both of my fathers. So I called Poorer Dad, but his phone had been disconnected. So you know what I did? I purchased the Enron stock at $77 a share, and when that stock value eventually reached zero, I no longer had to worry about a future market crash. Now, every night, whether the Dow closes up or down, I sleep like a baby!

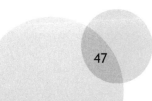

How I Turned $50,000 Cash into Eleven Beanie Babies

Remember when Beanie Babies were all the rage? People were taking out second mortgages to afford the cuddly little things. But then Beanie Babies started showing up on the "marked down" tables at flea markets and swap meets. The plush toys, some of which once sold for $3,000 each, now seemed to be available at 2 for $10 in some sale bins. And then folks began taking a good, hard look at the furry little creatures, and they realized they'd been paying thousands of dollars for something that looked rather ordinary. They were cute, but those Beanies didn't even talk, have mechanical movements, or hug you back. And now they were dropping in price like beachfront property after a tidal wave.

Some people were wise enough to sell off their Beanie Baby holdings just in time. Then there are us folks in that other group—the Beanie-Baby debtors—forced to tell our children, "Sorry, Timmy, there's no money for college. However, you can spend the next four years looking at this!" And we'd shove that overpriced Beanie in Timmy's face and watch his tears of disappointment suddenly turn to joy at the cuddliness of it. Who needs college when you have a $50,000 investment in eleven Beanie Babies now worth $112.48? It doesn't take a college education to understand that mathematical problem. But they're soooooo cute!

Factoid
If a monkey sat in front of a typewriter, hitting the keys at random, some speculate he might eventually write a self-help book.

The Deadbeat Next Door

We surveyed five hundred deadbeats from across the nation to get a feel for their lifestyles, their habits, the way they make their investment decisions, and how they became the deadbeats they are today.

Of the five hundred surveys we mailed out to certified deadbeats, more than four were returned. From this we gleaned the following results:

- Deadbeats usually do not have doctoral degrees; and if they do, they're from some place like Ed's University.

- Deadbeats are often named Norm, Larry, Spike, or Sally.

- Deadbeats favor pencils over pens. In some instances, crayons.

- Three out of four deadbeats rank "sleeping" as their favorite activity.

- Deadbeats often make poor life decisions, such as

skipping the SAT test to stay home and watch the Lotto drawing on TV.

- Deadbeats are poor goal setters.

- Deadbeats frequently blow off authors taking surveys.

We learned other important facts from our survey as well. For instance, we found that deadbeats often are procrastinators, that they like to gamble, and although they don't drink green tea, they sometimes will wear green shirts. And they all seem to have ten fingers (but only three out of four have ten toes).

Sea-Monkeys: The New Google

They're baaaaaaack—Sea-Monkeys!

We pride ourselves on going against the grain and finding value in out-of-favor investments. As contrarian thinkers in the world of finance, it's important to root out those hidden treasures, those overlooked nuggets, the dogs, the downtrodden, and ridiculed investment opportunities. And let's be honest, few things have fallen more out of widespread favor than the Sea-Monkeys market.

When was the last time you saw an ad for these homely little critters in the back of a magazine? Admit it, it's been years! Our research indicates that the only place one can find ads for Sea-Monkeys now are in thirty-year-old magazines in a dentist's waiting room.

But we say the wise investor looks beyond today's stocks, real estate, bonds, and commodities, and looks to yesterday. The smart, nostalgic investor will put his or her fortune in Sea-Monkeys.

Based on past performance, we're sure these simians of the petri dish will vastly outperform other investment classes in coming years. Sea-Monkeys are primed for a comeback—just like eight-track tapes and beta video recorders.

But don't just take our word for it. Let's compare the growth potential of Sea-Monkeys with the growth potential of other investment options. For example, real estate: To build a home takes many months. One must lay a foundation, pour concrete, add bricks and mortar, landscape the yard, and erect a porch large enough to accommodate three Avon representatives and six Jehovah's Witnesses all arriving at the same time on a Saturday afternoon.

What's required to grow a Sea-Monkey? You and a glass of water.

What about a start-up company? To form a corporation, you must have stockholders, a board of directors, and in some instances a shady, soon-to-be-indicted, corporate CEO.

How do you start a Sea-Monkey company? Mail in the order form.

If this doesn't prove to you that Sea-Monkeys are the investment opportunity of opportunities, that they are your ship just waiting to come in, we don't know what does.

Sea-Monkeys are the Google of tomorrow, the Berkshire Hathaway of the new millennium, the Magellan Fund of the next market wave. We're in a modern-day gold rush, and the gold you're panning for is spelled S-e-a-M-o-n-k-e-y-s. Bet the farm, mortgage the house, buy low and sell high. In the coming decade a "diversified portfolio" will be one equally divided between four sizes of Sea-Monkeys. Act now and be on the cutting edge of Wall Street!

Best of all, as far as we know and as of right now, Sea-Monkeys are a no-load investment, meaning you don't pay any broker or commission fees. So make your investment today. The future of the worldwide economy is shouting, SEA-MONKEY!! And for a limited time only, it's a buyer's market.

One day soon the list of wealthiest people could read:

1. Bill Gates, Microsoft founder

2. Warren Buffett, stock-market investor

3–6. The Walton Family, Wal-Mart stores

7. [Your name here], Sea-Monkeys

8. Larry Ellison, Oracle

Don't let fame and fortune pass you by . . . again!

5 Signs You've Chosen a Bad Financial Advisor

1. To fund a secure retirement, he suggests you fight Mike Tyson.

2. At your initial meeting, he wears an electronic ankle bracelet so the police know his whereabouts.

3. He always calls you collect from pay phones.

4. In lieu of stocks, bonds, and cash, his investment vehicles are Bingo and tossing coins into wishing wells.

5. He loses much of your life savings in the market: he drops the money while shopping in the supermarket.

Real-Estate Investing

Sure, real-estate prices tend to run in cycles, and this may or may not be a good time to buy. But who are you going to listen to: the experts or the fast-talking, overanxious Realtor looking to unload a $500,000 two-bedroom home next door to a meth lab?

The Realtor, of course! After all, if people always used wisdom and caution when it came to real-estate investments, who'd ever be able to get rich off of them? The world needs investors like us: people who will pay top dollar for a property just before the market collapses; visionaries who don't mind getting doused when the bubble bursts. We're the ones who keep even the most unscrupulous of Realtors in business. We're the ones who write checks to all those phony home-repair salesmen. We're the trusting souls who give out our checking-account number, credit-card number (and PIN), and other personal information to total strangers who call us in the middle of the night, because after all, "they seemed so nice." Without us, how could any of these hardworking, dedicated shysters make a decent living? They certainly wouldn't be able to vacation in Tahiti or the Caribbean.

Or send their kids to the best colleges. And then how could we live with ourselves?

8 Signs You've Moved into a Bad Neighborhood

1. The welcome wagon is carjacked.

2. You learn that the beautiful, quiet, serene park adjacent to your property is actually a federally protected peacock breeding facility.

3. You wake up the first morning and find gang graffiti spray-painted on your forehead.

4. The neighborhood is well lit . . . due to the fifteen police helicopters constantly circling overhead.

5. As you pull into your driveway with the moving truck, you're greeted with, "Hi, I'm your next-door neighbor. Do you like my new instrument? It's the world's largest tuba."

6. The first morning, as you leave your garage, two guys offer to clean your windshield with a squeegee.

7. The FBI asks if they can use your new home to conduct a stakeout until escrow closes on it.

8. You find out that "Neighborhood Watch" means your neighbors frequently press their faces to your windows to see inside.

5 Signs You're Represented by the Wrong Real-Estate Professional

1. He gets people to show up for the open house by raffling off your possessions.

2. When you ask her why she accepted the buyer's $200,000 offer on your appraised $350,000 home, she says, "I was afraid my cell phone was about to cut out."

3. Instead of encouraging a thorough inspection of the house you're about to purchase, he suggests you "just skip it and roll the dice."

4. Instead of your Realtor's photo on a bus bench, you see your actual Realtor sitting on a bus bench all day long, waving at passing cars.

5. Instead of using the Internet, her "property search" involves the use of an assessor's map and a divining rod.

5 Good Reasons to List Your Property Yourself

1. You won't have as many people traipsing through your house and criticizing your decorating taste (or the tree growing out of the dust on your coffee table).

2. You can save a bucketload of money.

3. You can save a bucketload of money.

4. You can save a bucketload of money.

5. You can save a bucketload of money.

How to Know You Paid Too Much for Your Home

- After winning an intense bidding war, you learn the "other party" you were bidding against was your wife on the downstairs phone.

- Your down payment is presented to the bank on one

of those six-by-twelve-foot checks they give at charity fund-raisers.

- You pay $50,000 over the list price because you're told the home was "formerly owned by Hollywood royalty." After moving in, you open a cabinet and find several of Carrot Top's old props.

- You receive a letter from the bank stating that they refuse to grant the loan unless it's cosigned by Warren Buffett.

- You begin to suspect the reason that hole in the backyard is called an "infinity pool" is because that's when you'll be done paying for it.

- An asterisk and corresponding note written in fine print indicate that the comparative market analysis was tabulated for homes the same size as yours but made of solid gold.

7 Signs You've Made a Bad Real-Estate Investment

1. The words "as is" appear 749 times in the contract.

2. The home warranty expires in thirty-six hours. And that's the extended warranty.

3. During the final walk-through, the home inspector falls through a hole in the roof. And on the insurance report, you have to clarify which hole.

4. The crown moldings turn out to be made of actual mold.

5. The sellers apparently did not realize the toilets and doorknobs were part of the deal and took them all with them.

6. The address is 4369 San Andreas Fault Drive.

7. That almanac-sized bundle of paper the sellers left behind turns out to be the final disclosure statement.

How to Turn a Million Dollars in Real Estate into $187,000 in Cash

First, buy your house in an overinflated housing market.

Second, waive your home inspection. In the thirty-five minutes it takes to conduct an inspection, you could miss out on the deal of a lifetime.

If the property is a fixer-upper, all the better. *Fixer-upper* is a technical real-estate term meaning "enlarged outhouse." Not only will you be paying a million dollars for a place that's tiny and dilapidated and, in a realistic market, worth maybe $19,500 tops, but you'll be sinking even more money into the property to bring everything up to city codes—like adding a roof and indoor plumbing.

Next, contact your mortgage lender. These are the most trustworthy individuals around, and they would never do or say anything that did not benefit you 100 percent. You can trust them! If they offer "prime plus 20 percent, hidden closing costs, 12-percent broker fees, balloon payment (a balloon big enough to sail around the world in) due in two years" and recommend a title company that collects a $4,000 kickback fee for the Realtor, it's a good deal for you! Just sign on the dotted line.

Then, once the property is yours, simply wait for the real-estate market to crash. When it does, put your place on the market and watch the lowball offers start pouring in!

Retire at Age Ninety-Five? Yes, You Can!

Tired of the workday grind? Long commute and rat race got you down? Sick of office politics? Want to take your job and send it back where it came from? Well, now you can! You don't have to be like all those other poor slobs who work until they're one hundred just to get that coveted gold watch. Thanks to the retirement tips provided in our book, you can now retire at age ninety-five and be the envy of all your friends! Imagine it—retiring while you're still young enough to do everything you could do at ninety-four! By following our proven methods of saving, investing, and spending less, it really is feasible to live out your dream of an early retirement.

Impossible, you say? You're not saving anywhere near the kind of money it would take for you to afford to retire at ninety-five? Don't worry. Nobody is. But that's what makes this the land of opportunity. A recent survey found that the typical American has $1.79 socked away for retirement. If you can just manage to save, say, two whole bucks (as one of the authors is close to saving), then in comparison with everyone else with their measly $1.79, you'll be the wealthy one! See how that works? Two bucks doesn't sound like a lot of money to retire on, but when everyone around you is 21 cents broker than you, you'll feel rich, and that's really what's important.

So don't get locked into thinking your only option is to work in your present profession until age eighty-five and then go to work as a Wal-Mart greeter* until you gasp your last breath. Start saving today!

Alternative Methods of Funding an Early and Happy Retirement

If you're willing to be a little creative, there are lots of ways to help fund your retirement. For example, over the years a number of proud Americans have sued fast-food establishments for making them fat and serving hot beverages that these people promptly spilled on themselves, earning a payday of around $5 million.

Despite current legislation designed to make it difficult to sue the fast-food giants for lavalike beverages or the inability to fit into our jeans after years of voluntarily ordering "fries with that," we're confident that this restrictive ruling will be overturned. So confident are we that we've included litigation as part of our recommended retirement plan. Suing fast-food companies for making us obese or for scalding us with piping hot beverages that we ourselves have ordered "hot"—as in "hot coffee" or "hot tea"— is the missing link to financial security and the high standard of living many of us seek in retirement.

But this is merely one option. You might also want to be on the lookout for other opportunities to beef up your retirement savings.

*There is absolutely nothing wrong with being a Wal-Mart greeter. We just want you to know there are plenty of other opportunities for older workers. You just have to look for them.

Chapter 2

"Caution—wet floor" signs are an almost certain bet that financial independence (and a neck and back brace) are in your future.

"How am I driving?" bumper stickers are a potential plethora of financial opportunity as well, and these are too often overlooked as a good source of financial supplement. "Uh . . . your employee cut me off on Interstate 40, causing me extreme mental duress. Duress in the neighborhood of, oh, say $200,000?"

Hard Hat Required signs are another oft-neglected source of income. "Oops, I didn't see the Hard Hat Required sign. It was blocked by my illegally parked SUV, and when I walked by your building, I was hit on the head with a small piece of wood falling from the scaffolding, allowing me to reach into the deep pockets of your construction company for, oh, how does $75,000 per splinter sound? I seem to have garnered ten of them. That's $750,000. Hmm, I guess they were right—the housing boom really can make a person rich!"

Beware of Dog signs might as well read, "Beware of lawsuit, buddy, because your pit bull pup just barked at me, scaring me and emotionally scarring me to the tune of $20,000."

Then there's the ol' "frog's head in the burger" trick. While totalitarian legislators seem bent on keeping us from suing fast-food restaurants for making us fat, they don't seem to mind us claiming we found something gross and disgusting in our burger or chili. No one is going to suspect an eighty-year-old woman of planting a cockroach or severed human finger in her food for the settlement money. And that's what makes it so perfect! This claim can provide the funds necessary to whisk you off to the Bahamas as soon as you hit your ninety-fifth birthday (after your fifteen-year court battle), freeing you to join the relaxed world of the retired.

And don't forget the Millionaires' Dating Service. Can we say retirement bonanza? A dating service designed for lonely millionaires? Please, this is like shooting ducks in a row—your ticket to love at first sight. First sight of his or her savings book, that is, and stock portfolio, and mansion, and Mercedes . . .

These are but a few of the ways a suit-savvy person can boost his or her retirement fund. And if the above suggestions don't work, just drown your retirement woes in some hot coffee with supersized fries, on us!

A Realistic Look at Where Your Retirement Monies Will Come From

Even if your $1.79 savings seems like twice what you're living on now, after credit-card payments, gas for your vehicle, taxes, and utility bills, it's not nearly enough to get you on that path toward precenturian retirement. So you're going to need some additional sources of income. Here's a chart that may help you know where your retirement income will come from:

Source of Retirement Income	Portion of Retirement Income
Dividends on investments	49.999999%
Social Security	.0000001%
Miscellaneous	.0000009%
Settlements from frivolous lawsuits	50%

We've already discussed ways to supplement your retirement income through litigation. Now let's examine the other three options.

Chapter 2

Dividends on Investments

This is the backbone of your retirement portfolio. A series of diversified, dividend-paying stocks and bonds will supply you with a steady stream of income.

As far as stocks go, we strongly urge you to stay away from anything with the words "dot-com." For example, in the 2000 market meltdown we were burned by what appeared to be solid companies with monikers like PlayItAgainFloss.com, Pet-Monkeys.com, and gravel.com.net. But buyer beware! Even though an investment sounds like a sure moneymaker, it could still spell trouble down the road. For help with your investment strategy, see "The RPS Method" later in this chapter.

Social Security

You may be counting on Social Security to make a significant contribution to your lifestyle in your twilight years. However, as we've already noted in the previous chart, we estimate that the portion of your retirement income that will come from Social Security will be only .0000001 percent.

Now, you're no doubt thinking, *But I've been paying into this system my entire life. Where did all my money go?!*

Exactly.

Clearly, as you can again see from our chart, the bulk of your retirement monies will come from dividend income and frivolous lawsuits. You should only count on Social Security to provide for a minuscule portion of your retirement living expenses—about as much as you make returning empty recyclable bottles and cans to the supermarket.

The main problem with Social Security isn't the program. It's the fact that we've naively put our trust in it. Most of us paid our hard-earned money into the Social Security program all of our working life, believing it would be there for us when we needed it. So quite frankly, the fault lies with us. What were we thinking? Just because the government was keeping track of how much our checks should be in retirement didn't mean we would ever actually see those checks. It's like playing Monopoly. It's play money. If we start thinking we actually own Boardwalk and Park Place and start listing them on our balance sheets, then we, it can be argued, are the silly gooses.

Miscellaneous

A small portion of your income during retirement will consist of earnings from various sorts of work. When you reach age eighty, you'll be eligible for employment at a fast-food restaurant—provided your reflexes are slow enough—or as a greeter at Wal-Mart. Due to the ever-rising cost of living, many retirees also supplement their income by raiding wishing wells or fountains at shopping malls or by looting the coin returns of pay phones. This has nothing to do with their ability to work.

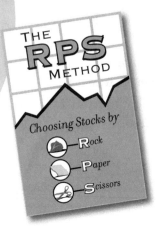

The RPS Method: Choosing Stocks by Rock, Paper, Scissors

Sure, you've tried all the investment strategies: the buy-and-hold philosophy, the market-timing philosophy, the contrarian philosophy. But did any of these methods work consistently? Let us answer that for you. No! It's never been a bull market for you, has it? All you've done is lose money on Wall Street, and you don't understand what you're doing wrong. Well, fret no more. After months of secret testing, we hereby introduce the one stock-selection strategy sure to beat all others: the Rock, Paper, Scissors Method.

This easy-to-learn method for making winning stock choices will revolutionize your world. Let's hear from a satisfied customer:

> As hard as it is to fathom, five years ago, before Brad and
> Martha developed the Rock, Paper, Scissors Method of picking
> stocks, I [unnamed rich person] was living in a ramshackle one-
> bedroom apartment on the wrong side of the tracks. Today, after
> diligently following the RPS Method, I live in a ramshackle
> two-bedroom apartment on the wrong side of the tracks!

Afraid you can't do it? Think Rock, Paper, Scissors is too difficult or challenging for a graduate of the public school system? We scoff at any such suggestion! By consistently applying yourself and regularly practicing the RPS Method, you, too, can one day move into a two-bedroom, wrong-side-of-the-tracks abode! Here's how it works:

1. Choose a stock from the business section of the newspaper. Say, for example, Poppa Tires.

2. With your hands, do the Rock, Paper, Scissors maneuver. Say rock comes up. Rock beats scissors.

3. Now move on to the next stock, say, Big Boned Clothes, and do the RPS maneuver again. Scissors beats paper. Move on to the next stock, and so on. Pretty soon, through the sheer process of elimination, you'll find your stock, and . . . voilá! You'll be raking in the dividends!

So if you're really serious about your desire to retire before the age of one hundred, throw away your *Wall Street Journal*, toss out your *New York Times*, turn off all those business shows on your television. They're passé, yesterday's news, old school! Rock, Paper, Scissors is the stock-picking wave of the future, and you've got to get on and ride it to Luxury Shore!

We are so confident that you'll soon see prognosticators on CNBC, the Fox business block, and all the other networks actually doing Rock, Paper, Scissors right on the air that we'll stake our PlayItAgainFloss.com stocks on it!

Unfortunately, the length of this book precludes us from describing the RPS Method in greater detail, mapping out the different strategies involved within the system, but we urge you

Chapter 2

to get our free pamphlet and CD, *Creating Wealth the Rock, Paper, Scissors Way*. (To obtain this free pamphlet and CD, simply send $199.95 for postage and handling to the authors of this book, and we—er, you—will soon be on your way to obscene riches!)

Daily Affirmations for the Deadly Dull

1. I can throw caution to the wind and do something outrageously daring—today I'm ordering French fries for lunch instead of onion rings!

2. I speak with such enthusiasm that my friends will have to stop referring to me as "the walking snooze alarm."

3. I have a dynamic personality. Motivational speakers will no longer throw up their hands and walk out of the room when I enter.

4. The only reason people yawn in my presence is because I'm checking their molars.

5. I can find a new hobby. Collecting Dixie cups just lacks a certain pizzazz.

6. If I'm patient, people whose cataracts have simply fallen away from their eyes from all the rubbing and blinking they do during conversations with me will one day thank me for their restored sight.

7. I can be the life of the party . . . just as soon as I get invited to one.

8. Not everyone is in a coma because of something I said.

9. I am more exciting than watching paint dry. Or at least as exciting.

10. I am not dull! I am not dull! I am not . . . zzzzzzzz.

Maybe Your Body's Just Not That Into You

Chapter 3

Live to 120 and Beyond!

Unless your quality of life has been so severely diminished that you're only receiving three channels on your television (none of them in your own language), your camcorder is the size of a microwave oven, and the last new release you watched was *King Kong* (the original film), you, like everyone else, probably want to live to be 120. But desire isn't the only thing you'll need in order to arrive at your supergolden years. You'll need to start now taking some definitive steps toward that goal.

In reality, only a handful of us will ever see, much less blow out, 120 candles on our birthday cake. But we at the Evergreen Life Extension Society are seeking to increase that number, because we take long life spans seriously. We believe that living to 120 and beyond is not only achievable but will one day be commonplace. True, occasionally a little speed bump is thrown in our path—like last year when the president of our society died in San Francisco at age fifty-two after being run over by a trolley on his way home from the seminar "How to Live Forever." Unfortunately, he never saw the trolley coming, and because of his untimely death, the seminar had to be renamed "How to Cross a Street."

But aside from this one unfortunate event, we believe that by following a few simple rules, anyone can extend his or her life span while simultaneously enjoying a productive, happy existence.

Living a long life has many advantages. Consider just a few:

- You can officially say you've exceeded the shelf life of fruitcake.

- You'll finally pay off that $500 credit-card purchase you made back in 1979.

- You get to spend the money from your own estate.

- You get to attend all your enemies' funerals.

- You'll still be alive when the cable guy shows up for the appointment you made in 1997.

Of course, to fully enjoy the advantages of a long life, the first step is to achieve long life. The following guidelines will help make this possible.

1. Subsist almost entirely on tree bark and sunflower seeds

Studies have shown that consuming fewer calories prolongs your life. We at the Evergreen Life Extension Society firmly believe that the most effective way to accomplish this is by eating nothing but bark and seeds, with a tiny bit of alfalfa sprouts every third Thanksgiving.

2. Never leave your home

Repeated studies have shown that while many accidents occur inside the home, it's the people who leave their homes who are at greatest risk. Thus, aside from attending the Live to Be 120 seminars, always remain inside your house or apartment, with the windows and doors locked. Once every couple of years it may be necessary to go out to purchase large supplies of food, and possibly ammunition. With that exception, never leave your home!

3. Never kiss anyone (even on the cheek)

Studies have shown kissing is a potential purveyor of disease. Instead, if you truly care about another person, a good firm handshake while wearing a double layer of latex gloves will suffice. If you must, draw hearts on the glove.

4. Never, ever watch the news or read the newspaper

The news is always depressing, and exposure to it can lead to depression. And that's even more depressing. So why read a newspaper or watch a news program on TV? It'll just get you down. The last time we read a newspaper, the headline was, "Dewey Defeats Truman," and we haven't watched TV news since Cronkite retired.

5. Avoid stress

Set up a hammock in your basement and spend all your waking hours in contemplation. We also recommend building a small fire in a fireplace or other safe indoor fire container and rolling up all your monthly bills for makeshift fire logs.

7 Secret Keys to Weight Loss

1. Do not eat food that has to be baled. (Or at least, don't have seconds.)

2. Don't drink anything from a convenience store that's in a cup the size of a 747. The size of a small prop plane is acceptable.

3. Take small bites (you should have to chomp into that Big Mac at least three times before it disappears).

4. Begin your exercise program after, and only after, your cholesterol reading comes up and the numbers are the largest since Steven Hawking took the SAT.

5. Stop gnawing on this page.

6. Marry a person twice your size so you'll seem thin by comparison.

7. Have your stomach loosely stitched. Stapling, while growing in popularity, is a drastic measure. Loose stitching allows the occasional brownie to sneak through.

The Worry Weight-Loss Plan

It's here! The breakthrough, runaway diet revolution! Throw away those low-carb cookbooks, those stair steppers, your treadmill, and all those diet pills! The new millennium's latest diet plan? Losing weight through worry.

That's right—now your worry can do more than eat away the lining of your stomach! It can get you into that dress you've been wanting to wear for months. Here's how it works:

- Worrying about the widening hole in the ozone layer: 180 calories burned

- Worrying about the widening, lumpy mound that was once your waistline: 240 calories burned

- Worrying about the potential of a President Arnold Schwarzenegger: 114 calories burned

- Picturing yourself on a Carnival cruise ship surrounded by five hundred passengers who've just consumed the midnight buffet (all of it), when acute dysentery strikes: 490 calories burned

- The thought of Supreme Court Justice Judge Judy: 600 calories burned

- Imagining the words, "Mom, Dad, I'd like you to meet my husband, Mondo, the tattooed biker. Hope you don't mind that we eloped": 750 calories burned

- Picturing an envelope marked "Greetings from the IRS!" arriving in your mailbox: 1,350 calories burned

Factoid
Frequently the
self-help bandwagon
rides on two wheels.

The Latkins Diet Revolution

Tired of all that beef and poultry in your diet? Looking for some other forms of protein to help you stay on your low-carb diet? Here are some meal-plan suggestions:

Day 1

Breakfast: Half a hog's head, dipped in butter and covered with twelve pounds of bacon; side dish of four pounds of cheese, preferably gouda

Lunch: Six-inch helping of walrus tongue, followed by pickled possum feet and a spinach-and-leek quiche

Dinner: One-half whale carcass plus the hindquarters of a feral pig, and one fish cracker

Day 2

Breakfast: Eighteen inches of broiled monkey claw covered with thick raccoon gravy and topped with half a fried muskrat's nose

Lunch: Ten pounds of broiled venison and a sprig of parsley

Dinner: Fourteen-pound strip of raw pig guts and twelve biscuits (for garnish only)

Day 3

Repeat meal plan from day 1.

Day 4

Repeat meal plan from day 2.

Day 5

Breakfast: Two heaping bowls of singed skunk innards and a sippy cup of orange juice
Lunch: Leg of equine
Dinner: Sautéed goat liver and a rack of roasted ribs half the size of a Mini Cooper (no barbecue sauce)

Day 6

Breakfast: Filleted sheep ears, sixteen strips of bacon, and a small triangle of pita bread
Lunch: Supersized fried eel sandwich (with light mayo)
Dinner: One squirrel, roasted, no acorns, and a large glass of ox milk

Day 7

Breakfast: Pork chops, possum sausage, and two hams
Lunch: Three arms of squid and one cup of gristle
Dinner: Deer intestines, grilled armadillo, and broiled lizard tail, with an olive for dessert
(Caution: These are not actual diet suggestions, these are jokes; don't eat this stuff! It would be bad for you. Tasty, but really, really bad.)

The Tapeworm Diet

Why go to all the bother of counting calories to lose weight? There's a better way. You've heard of personal trainers (PTs)? Well, our PT (personal tapeworm) can give you the same results, and you won't have to pay $75 per hour for it! More importantly, a personal tapeworm is far less nagging than a personal trainer. He's not going to shame you into doing a single push-up or running on a treadmill. In fact, he'd probably rather you just sit still and let him sleep.

So go on—eat everything you want, and don't think twice about it. Let your personal tapeworm do the work of digesting all those calories for you! Then, when you finally fit into that size six again, simply schedule an appointment with your doctor to have the tapeworm removed. Voilà! You're back to your dream weight, the tapeworm's free to see the sights, and your doctor's $2,000 richer—and all because you had that pioneer spirit and weren't afraid to try out this revolutionary new diet.

You might even want to pose for an "after" picture with your little PT. (We say "little," but your personal tapeworm may actually be the size of the Loch Ness monster, depending on how long and how often you've fed him. But who cares? You'll be shopping for single-digit sizes again and, other than some small intestinal scars, a little colon cleansing, and general discomfort, you'll be looking good!) And as for what to do with that "after" picture of you standing alongside your new, surgically removed friend . . . what better way to say Merry Christmas to all your friends and family!

10 Affirmations for the Overly Cynical

1. I can accomplish anything I want today! (Yeah, right.)

2. I love my job. It's just my boss, the work, my coworkers, and the hours that I hate.

3. I'm scheduled to get a raise next week, but I'll probably be dead by then.

4. I have many friends, and they all want a piece of me.

5. I can lose weight. Or gain it. But I am determined to change my destiny! Or not.

6. I can make a difference in the world, but why in the world would I want to?

7. Even though I'm joining a twelve-step program, I really only need eight of them.

8. I've never seen the sun shining so brightly. No, wait. That's just a nuclear power plant meltdown. Just my luck. No sunglasses.

9. This could be the start of something big . . . or a free fall down a deep chasm, never again to see the light of day.

10. The sky is falling! The sky is falling! Of course it is. Why would I expect anything less?

Why French Women Don't Get Hefty

Caffiene, Nicotine, and Other Things That Make You Go *Oui-Oui!*

Why French Women Don't Get Hefty

In a recent interview with four women of French descent, we gained insight into the French way of dieting. Here's what they had to offer.

Ever notice that we French women don't pack on the pounds like you Americans? We simply don't. As many of you Americans get bigger each year until you look like Goodyear blimps with tiny heads attached, we maintain our figures. And now you want to learn the secret of our success, why we are svelte and you are not? Well, we will tell you. Strangely, it has very little to do with our genes, our exercise habits, or how we prepare our food. We don't have any more will power than you Americans.

That we remain thin while you grow to grotesque proportions akin to wooly mammoths with glandular disorders, with all due respect, has to do with the fact that we are incredibly, outrageously rude.

Rude, us? Can you believe that? Well, can you, American?

I will try to explain, and I will try not to use any big words so as not to confuse you.

When dining out, we frequently take a small bite of food and spit it out, right into the waiter's face. "Take this back to the kitchen, you filthy American swine!" we shout, as the helpless waiter scampers back to the kitchen.

We then demand to speak with the chef. When the chef appears, we immediately blow a puff of smoke in his face. (We're not even smoking cigarettes. We just emit smoke when we yell.)

"That food should be buried eight feet underground, only I fear it may kill all the worms and taint the water supply, your cooking is so abhorrent!" we tell the chef.

The chef usually goes and gets Security. As soon as we spot these men in uniform, we immediately surrender to them—after all, we are French. Soon French women are shown the door, without our even coming close to finishing our meal. This is how we maintain our slender French figures. Now leave us alone, you twit!

Of Course They're Experts, They're Famous Aren't They?

The Big Celebrity-Endorsed Diet

Celebrities often lend their names to certain diet or exercise plans. The celebrity looks great (though sometimes via other means, such as cosmetic surgery), and he or she will sell the unsuspecting television audience an exercise video and vitamins for $19.99 if they call within the next ten minutes. Those "ten minutes" often are allowed to stretch out for about four and a half years, or whenever the FDA cracks down on the company.

Our "big celebrity," whose diet and exercise tips we feature on the next page, hasn't enlisted the help of any plastic surgeons or used any other outside means to look great. She got in shape by simply following certain diet and exercise tips that she is all too willing to share with our readers.

Thank you, Brad and Martha, for giving me this opportunity to share my health and fitness secrets with the world. Or at least the four people who've bought your book.

Before I begin, however, I would like to say that even though I have name recognition, I am appearing on these pages incognito due to contractual agreements that might arise when I get offered my next movie deal. Do you think for one minute that I would be doing infomercials and writing diet and fitness tips in a book that will probably never even get on the *New York Times* Mediocre Selling List if I had a hot career going right now? And part of the blame falls to you, the buying

public. Had you purchased one of my old movies instead of this book, producers would see that there is a groundswell of interest in my work and offer me a job. But no, you bought another self-help book instead, to help yourself! You didn't even think about me! You haven't thought about me in fifteen years! I gave you the best years of my life, and this is the thanks I get? I had to sell my home in Malibu overlooking the ocean and am now renting an apartment in Pacoima overlooking an unfinished furniture factory and a taco/sushi stand, but do you care? No! But Brad Pitt and Angelina Jolie movies you can't get enough of!

That said, and to prove there are no hard feelings, I will now show you how you can make the most of your life by having the body of your dreams . . .

Big Celebrity Diet Tip #1

Gain weight. It makes losing weight much more meaningful.

Eat plenty of foods containing calories. Foods high in calories include fried chicken (with skin), movie-theater popcorn with extra butter, banana splits, and egg rolls.

Foods high in fat include sweet rolls, crème brûlée, and bacon. Foods high in cholesterol include barbecued ribs and pork sausage. These are foods you should eat plenty of. Bon appétit.

Big Celebrity Diet Tip #2

Now that you're at least twenty pounds overweight and your cholesterol level is through the roof, you're the perfect candidate for my weight-loss program. On this diet you should stay away from certain foods. These include fried chicken (with skin), movie-theater popcorn with extra butter, banana splits, and egg rolls. Foods high in fat include sweet rolls, crème brûlée, and bacon. Foods high in cholesterol include barbecued ribs and pork sausage. Do not eat another bite of these foods!

Big Celebrity Diet Tip #3

In addition to the three food groups—calories, fat, and cholesterol— there is another group of food that's often overlooked: condiments. Condiments include such tasty fare as salt, sugar, ketchup, and caviar. Not only are condiments good for you, but they come already packaged in healthy serving sizes. For example, just add twelve packets of sugar to your cup of coffee, and you're good to go.

Big Celebrity Diet Tip #4

Have some more condiments. And while we're on the subject of that Jared guy from the Subway sandwich shops (OK, we weren't really talking about him, but I wanted to bring him up), this guy apparently lost a lot of weight eating Subway sandwiches every day. Now he's all over the TV promoting himself. This is valuable airtime that should go to me! But I digress . . .

Big Celebrity Diet Tip #5

Consume nothing but caffeine for one week. Taking in nothing but caffeine for seven days straight can really make the pounds fall off. I discovered this by accident in 1983, when I was cast as the lead in a coffee commercial and was on the set fourteen hours a day for an entire week. I lost twelve pounds! I had no idea an uncontrollable twitch could burn up that many calories.

And there you have it. All the health knowledge I've gained through my thirty years in the entertainment industry. For additional tips, please look for my new diet book, *Diet Tips from a Hungry Diva*, to be released in summer 2010.

The Toxin Diet

Why waste time detoxing your system when you can lose weight and have the body of your dreams with the Toxin Diet? The Toxin Diet allows you to eat all the toxins you want and never worry about weight gain, thanks to the subsequent intestinal problems. Though not yet approved by the FDA, the Toxin Diet is gaining widespread underground support.

Diet the Heimlich Way!

The Heimlich Diet is growing in popularity, and it's easy to see why. On the Heimlich Diet you can eat all you want. The secret lies in eating too fast and then choking. Not to the point of passing out—just to the point of causing a scene until someone helps you reject that lodged food item and send it sailing across the room.

Obviously, this diet isn't for everyone. But if you're one of those folks who can cough loud enough or give the international choking signal clearly, so someone at a neighboring table will rush to your aid, this just might be the diet you're looking for! And best of all, after the calorie-filled food is dislodged, you'll have the whole restaurant cheering for you as the color returns to your face and you start eating again.

What other diet affords you that kind of support? Plus, if you're single and your rescuer happens to be a single person of the opposite sex, who knows what kind of lasting relationship could develop from this chance meeting? Cinderella may have had her slipper to leave behind for Prince Charming, but that's nothing compared to the romance of a flying chunk of beef hitting the side of a would-be suitor's head.

Abs, Who Needs 'Em?

Are washboard abs really all that attractive? Or have we been sold a bill of goods? We say it's the latter. We say abs are passé. We say the latest look isn't the washboard stomach but rather a stomach that looks like a lumpy, bulging laundry bag.

Factoid
Some self-help authors are looked down upon by people who write pop-up books.

The Ultimate Celebrity Workout

For those of us who need to combine diet and exercise, we offer the Ultimate Celebrity Workout.

The cornerstone of my fitness program consists of exercise and diet. My exercise routine is complex and difficult, so please check with your physician before beginning anything this rigorous!

Pinky Roll

We'll start with the pinky roll. This firms and tones the little finger. Simply lift your pinky one-half inch, then return to the resting position.

Nose Lift

This is called the Nose Lift. It tones the nasal cavity. It's important to protect my nose—I paid good money for it.

Hairbrush Row

The Hairbrush Row develops the triceps, which is somewhere on the upper half of your body—or it may be a suburb of Peoria. I'll have to check with my personal trainer . . .

Telescope

I call this one the Telescope. It flexes the fingers and forearms. Ladies, go easy on this one; you don't want those arm muscles getting too developed!

Squat

Here I'm doing the Squat. This strengthens the entire lower body.

Floss Till You Drop

I call this move Floss Till You Drop. I love to do it to a disco beat. How exhilarating! Floss left, floss right! This exercise develops the biceps and shoulder muscles.

In all my exercises, I do two sets of one rep each, and then I head for a hot sauna. Or a waiting ambulance. Either way, it feels great!

Natural Cures "The Man" Doesn't Want You to Know About

Forget everything you know about medical science and health. It's all right, we'll wait . . .

OK, have you forgotten? Good. Because we want to tell you about a fantastic, new, breakthrough way of looking at health and medicine!

Follow along with this step-by-step guide as we teach you how to cure yourself of any ailment known to man—including monkeypox, SARS, and avian flu!

Headache

Remember the not-so-good-old days when you used to pop an aspirin for a headache and had to wait for it to work? Did it? Probably more times than not, it didn't. So why are we still treating headaches in this manner? Instead, why not try this treatment for a headache: Spread two ounces of witch hazel across a Graham cracker covered with light bark from a weeping-willow tree. Chew it slowly and swallow. Your headache should disappear within the hour! If it doesn't, hit yourself with this book fifty times until you lose consciousness and sleep off your headache. (We're just kidding about the witch hazel and weeping-willow bark. The graham cracker and hitting your head is fine.)

Toothache

Remember when you used to have to see a dentist when your tooth was throbbing and your cheek had swollen to twice its size? Well, thanks to the minutes of research that have gone into the writing of this book, those days are long gone! We suggest trying the natural, holistic approach to curing an aching tooth. Apply the sautéed liver of a bullfrog, and chase it with horseradish-and-pumpkin sauce. Wait two hours, then drink juice from an Eastern Mongolian banana tree. If this doesn't work, hit the swollen cheek with this book fifty times until that pain is substantially worse than the toothache.

Hemorrhoids

Sit in a bath of baking soda and camphor for thirty minutes while drinking apple cider brewed by a man named Jebediah. If that doesn't work, sit on this book for fifty minutes. This won't cure your hemorrhoids, but it will help flatten out all the pages again.

Poison Ivy

Cover the area with a coating of maple syrup and spring water from a Colorado stream, taken at high noon on a Tuesday (preferably with Morrie) in the third week of February in a year ending with a 3 or a 1. If that doesn't work, use the edges of this book to scratch across your rash at least fifty times.

Monkeypox, SARS, and Avian Flu

OK, we were just kidding. If you contact any of these, the only thing we can recommend with full confidence is that you stay at least fifty book lengths away from us!

10 Affirmations for the Procrastinator

1. Just do it! Whenever.

2. Now that I'm ninety-eight and have outlived most of the people in my hometown, this would be a great time to get my driver's license!

3. I can accomplish anything I want to accomplish if I would just finish what I . . .

4. (Twenty minutes later) Where was I? Oh, yes, I can accomplish anything I want to accomplish if I would just finish what I start. I control my destiny.

5. I never put off until tomorrow what I can do four weeks from now.

6. All good things come to those who wait . . . decades.

7. Today I will finally do something about that carton of milk in my refrigerator dated October 3, 1997. I'll push it to the back of the shelf and finish the carton marked May 14, 1995, first.

8. I no longer procrastinate on voting. First thing in the morning, I'm going to mail in that absentee ballot to elect Gore/Lieberman.

9. I am a good citizen. In fact, as soon as I'm done with this list, I'm going to return the library book I borrowed in 1968, face the music, and pay the $127,244.25 fine.

10. And lastly . . . Oh, never mind. I'm sure I'll come up with the last affirmation before this book goes to print. Or not.

Maybe Work's Just Not That Into You

Chapter 4

AN AMAZING WAY TO BLOCK CHANGE IN YOUR WORK AND IN YOUR LIFE

Who Moved My Doughnut?

Yes, change can be a blessing in rare circumstances, like when your house is on fire and you need to move out. But more often than not, it's a curse. It shakes your foundation, throws your entire world off balance, and can really ruin your day.

In *Who Moved My Doughnut?* we will introduce you to four characters who have had to adapt to change.

Smelly and Glazed are two mice who discover during the daily trip through their maze that someone has moved their doughnut (doughnut is a metaphor for doughnut).

The other two characters are Krispy and Kreme.* These two mouse-sized humans also find themselves searching for their doughnut. (You think you've got problems, try going through life being referred to as "a mouse-sized human.")

Smelly, Glazed, Krispy, and Kreme will need to modify some of their behaviors in order to survive in their altered environment—just as we all need to adapt to the changes in our work and life.

* No relation to the popular doughnut chain

Say your boss decides you no longer need your own private office and moves you to a broom closet. Do you sulk and send him or her rude, anonymous e-mails? Of course you do! Does it change anything? Of course it doesn't. You're still in your broom closet . . . but you do feel better because you vented.

Sometimes change is about stubbornness—about making the world go around you, being that stick in the mud that irritates everyone. Like Penny Whitaker, who held up construction of Interstate 40 by refusing to move her dilapidated mobile home and forcing the interstate to go around her home and through Bucksnort, Tennessee. She held out and to this day is living happily in her trailer, in the exact location where it's always been. We're not 100-percent sure this account is true, but why else would a major interstate go through a town called Bucksnort?

So what's the moral of this story? When change comes your way, resist. Tell it you were there first! Keep using those eight-track tapes no matter how many people are walking around with iPods. Walk into the video store and proudly ask for the beta section! Defiantly give your loved ones Pet Rocks at holidays. Don't go with the flow and change with the times—for goodness' sake, people, take a stand!

Schmooze Your Way to the Top

Much has been written about getting ahead in the world. What's generally overlooked is the power of kissing up. You think the big prizes in life go to those who persevere, work hard, and receive good educations? What cave have you recently emerged from? Getting ahead in the office is a matter of kissing up to the right people. We offer the following suggestions:

- Instead of buying Christmas presents for your spouse and children next year, pool all your money to buy the boss one great gift.

- In lieu of spending your weekends visiting your aging mother in the assisted-living center, opt to wash the boss's car or caddy for her on the golf course. Or maybe offer to bathe her Doberman. Those brownie points add up!

- Instead of passing on the name of your father or your spouse's father (or even your spouse), consider naming your firstborn after the boss. And not just the first name. If your boss's name is Arnold William Melon, consider naming your son Arnold William Melon [your last name here].

- Arrive at work early to dust the boss's parking space. Then, when he pulls into the space, shout, "You look very handsome today, Mr. [your boss's name here]."

- Keep your eyes open to see if the boss needs any little chores to be done. For example, if you happen to be passing by and your boss leans back in her chair, make a mad dash into her office and shove a footstool under her feet. If the boss doesn't have a footstool, throw your body onto the floor, allowing her to prop up her feet on your back.

- When you get an extra ticket to a ball game or the symphony, tell your wife she needs to look at the big picture, then leave her at home and take the boss.

- When the boss asks what you're planning to do on vacation, respond by saying, "What are you planning to do, sir?" No matter how ridiculous or obscure the boss's plans are—even if he's going lawn bowling in Australia—say, "My goodness, I don't believe it; that's what we're planning to do too!" Then quickly learn to lawn bowl.

By forgoing a solid education and hard work and devoting yourself to following these rules for kissing up—we mean schmoozing—you should soon find yourself at the top of the corporate world.

Floss for Success

Floss for Success is the newest self-help trend that finally proves, once and for all, that all the good ideas for self-improvement books were used up years ago. Here's the program:

Step One: Floss Your Way to Great Professional Relationships

As everybody knows, the key to a perfect business relationship is regular flossing. Start with a twice-a-day regimen, then increase to three times a day, and watch your relationships with coworkers improve dramatically overnight!

Step Two: Floss Your Way to Great Riches

Of course it's widely known that Bill Gates and Warren Buffett built their fortunes based mostly on regular flossing. You, too, can accumulate great wealth by flossing daily. Simply floss four times daily: once in the morning, twice in the afternoon, and once in the evening, and watch your bank account grow! Soon you will be living in the lap of luxury, and like all the millionaires who have flossed before you, you'll owe it all to the power of the floss.

Maybe Your Brain's Just Not That Into You

Chapter 5

The Power of Not Thinking at All

What gets most people into trouble is their thinking. Either their thinking is negative and causes them to inadvertently sabotage their own success, or it's positive and irritates everybody around them.

The power of both kinds of thinking can be debated. But what you don't hear much about is the power of not thinking at all. Political figures throughout history have practiced this method with remarkable results. We count ourselves among the great nonthinkers of the world, both past and present.

The Complete Moron's Guide to Being an Idiot

For those of you who think being an idiot is easy, think again. Or don't think again, as the case may be. For a true idiot, nothing is easy. It's a challenge to keep all those school books in mint condition by never opening them once and to ask all those dumb questions, like "Who's buried in Grant's tomb?" Everyone knows the answer to that. (It's empty. Amy Grant doesn't need a tomb yet—she's still very much alive.) And even though the smart students don't realize it, a true idiot takes his life in his hands every day when he falls asleep in chemistry class or at work—especially if there are dangerous chemicals nearby that might combust when mingled with drool.

Yes, being an idiot requires hard work and constant vigilance—even at home. You have to phone your cable company and have all public television manually blocked until someone comes out with an I-chip (idiot chip) to automatically block all intelligent programming. Fortunately, there are only a couple of hours of intelligent television programming, so not having the I-chip doesn't cause too much damage.

Chapter 5

Still, there is help for those who desire to raise their level of stupidity. Our *Complete Moron's Guide to Being an Idiot* will help you navigate your way through life and be the biggest idiot you can be. (For those of you pausing to look up *The Complete Moron's Guide to Being an Idiot* in the table of contents so you can go directly there, we'd just like to point out: you're reading it now.)

For years enterprising authors have made fortunes selling books to those of us with self-esteem so low that we have no problem waiting in line at the bookstore with an "Idiot" tome under our arm, basically shouting to the world, "Look at me! I can't seem to achieve Idiot status on my own—I need help!" So, sensing the confusion that might arise in trying to determine if you are indeed an idiot, we've created the ultimate idiot checklist.

The Complete Moron's Checklist for Being an Idiot

1. When leaving a public rest room, it's always a good idea to have a long piece of toilet tissue stuck to your shoe (at least ten squares), as this makes an immediate impression on all you meet, and it also dusts the lobby floor behind you.

2. If you're a man, begin each day by tucking your necktie into your pants. This will keep it out of your spaghetti and let the fashion world know you are a force to be reckoned with.

3. Ideal business investments for the idiot:
   a. Eight-track tapes (According to idiot insiders, these are poised for a comeback.)
   b. Cliff acreage (Anyone can own horizontal property, but it takes a true idiot to realize the investment potential of vertical land holdings.)

  c. Purebred pet rocks

  d. Snowmobile dealership in Miami

4. When attending an all-you-can-eat buffet, always stick your face directly into the bowls of food and start devouring the fine cuisine right there in line. This saves valuable time, and in the likely event you have a coughing attack, it will keep all those nasty germs off the glass awning.

5. Find a hobby. Some excellent hobbies for idiots:

  a. Entering hot-dog eating contests (Doing the Heimlich maneuver is a great way to meet new friends.)

  b. Collecting blank pieces of paper

  c. Uphill skiing

  d. Knitting sweaters for Chia Pets

6. Look in the mirror each day to be sure you have a fresh deposit of food stuck between your teeth. Wearing spinach two days in a row is considered a fashion faux pas in Idiotland.

7. Good comebacks for idiots:

  a. "You think this is stupid? I'll show you stupid!"

  b. "I'm nobody's fool! I'm a free agent."

  c. "What's my I.Q.? Like it matters!"

  d. "Back off, man! You don't know the kind of idiot you're messing with!"

8. Social tips for idiots:

  a. After a date, always walk the person to—wait, what are the odds of you having a date?

   b. Always arrive fashionably late to a party. Say, by three or four days.

   c. When talking on the telephone, try to always have a mouthful of celery. It immediately lets the other party know not only that you're an idiot but also that you're getting plenty of roughage in your diet.

   d. Always wait three years to call a potential date who gives you his or her phone number, so you don't appear needy. (See "How to Stay Single into Your Eighties.")

9. Suggested reading for idiots:
   a. T-shirt slogans
   b. Cereal boxes
   c. Rest room graffiti
   d. *Weekly World News,* alien-abduction section

10. Idiot's guide to the galaxy:
   a. Turn left
   b. Turn right
   c. Go straight
   d. All of the above

The Complete Moron's Guide to Handling Stress

Just the fact that you purchased this book and accept the truth that you have moronic tendencies speaks volumes as to how you handle stress. Let's take this step by step. We'll go slow.

Step 1

(To answer the question we're reasonably sure you're asking right now, we're beginning with one because one is the first number.) As a card-carrying member of the Moronic Society, you must absorb the truth that you are going to be put upon by many of those you meet. The reason for this is twofold: you have two ears, and you have precious little between them (at least in the way of common sense). Because of this you also will need to accept that your life will involve a certain misery. Once you do that, you can let go of stress. Don't worry about whether it's going to be a good day. "Have a nice day" doesn't apply to you. It will almost always be a stressful day.

Step 2

Recognize the three most common sources of stress for morons:

- Money (You can't keep much, and what you do keep around, you sometimes eat.)

- Relationships (Most of yours are with imaginary friends, and even they're not that impressed with you.)

- Family (Odds are, you're still waiting to get their forwarding address.)

Step 3

The main challenge for you is to lower your expectations immediately. Your daily goals should include the following:

- Getting all your shirt buttons aligned properly. (Forget the tie. Life's not that long.)

- Managing to catch the bus just once before it runs over your new sneakers.

- Not getting your fingers stuck in your trousers zipper.

- Getting through one entire day without finding a Kick Me sign stuck to your back.

The Complete Moron's Guide to Body Language

One of the best ways to know what another person is thinking is by interpreting his or her body language. Here are a few examples:

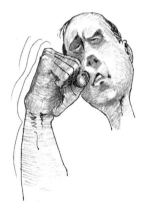

Translation: "I'd like to talk to you about a raise."

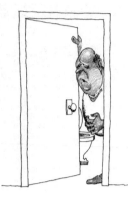

Translation: "Honey, your new rice dish is not quite to my liking."

Translation: "Confront who?"

Translation: "I'm sorry, but this seat is taken."

Excuse Me, Brotha, Your Life's Awaiting

Let us begin with this word from the wise: we get what we give. What we extend is what we receive back. To demonstrate, exhale . . . now inhale. See? Some of the same particles of air that you pushed out were sucked back in again! Probably some cold and flu viruses as well, but you get our point.

In the same way, sending out positive thoughts about others will bring positive thoughts back to you. And thinking negative thoughts about others will bring negative thoughts back to you. Thinking, *That guy is a jerk!* only brings more jerkiness into your life. Thinking, *That woman is a nut!* brings more nuts into your life. And so on. That's how it works. We receive what we send out.

Thinking the following negative, fearful thoughts will draw those negative, fearful things back to you.

Negative Thought: I hope I don't get hit by a truck.

Result: You get hit by a truck. Of course, it didn't help that you were doing your thinking in the middle of a busy intersection, but still—if you had been thinking positively, it might not have happened. And even if it did, you would have had a smile on your face when they took you away in the ambulance.

Negative Thought: I don't think I'd want to be eaten alive by a lion.

Result: A lion gets loose from the zoo, finds you sitting in your convertible at a red light thinking your negative thoughts, and the next thing you know, you're lion chow.

Negative Thought: I don't want to be buried by a twenty-ton mound of snow in an avalanche.

Result: Worst blizzard in U.S. history, and you're somewhere at the bottom of it.

Negative Thought: I don't want our kids to be dragged off into the woods by Bigfoot.

Result: Christmas-card photo now includes the hairy, seven-and-a-half-foot creature.

Negative Thought: I don't want to have our cable TV service go out.

Result: Anybody for a game of Monopoly?

By thinking these and other "don't wants," we're putting out fear vibes, and we end up drawing those exact events into our lives. Like the man we just read about last week who was continually thinking just such negative thoughts. Then one day he went for a walk and ended up being nearly killed by a twenty-ton avalanche of snow, after which he was attacked by a lion and his cable went out. But not all of his luck was bad. He did beat Bigfoot at Monopoly.

109 Affirmations for the Forgetful

1. Today is going to be a great day. Or was that yesterday?

2. I can introduce myself to five complete strangers today. Starting with me.

3. I can climb mountains, I can build bridges, I can sing songs . . . it's remembering where I live without having to look at my utility bill that gets a little tricky.

4. Today if I forget where I've parked my car, I won't stress over it. Especially if I've driven off in a better car.

5. No matter what else happens today, I will remember . . . something or other.

6. I radiate calm and inner peace, which is amazing considering I don't know where I left my wallet, my keys, my cell phone, or my spouse.

7. People flock to me—and I'm sure it's not just for the rewards I offer when they find something I've lost.

8. I am blessed to have a warm, close-knit family I get together with as often as possible. Unfortunately, they're not *my* family.

9. I had something really good for this one, if only I could remember it.

Unleash the Whiner Within

Are you one of those people who simply goes with the flow, who happily adjusts your sails to the wind so as not to rock any boats? Are you the "Don't make waves" type? Of course you are! That's why you've picked up this book. Well, we're here to tell you that it's time to change your ways!   Have you ever heard the saying, "The squeaky wheel gets the oil"? Truer words were never spoken. You've got to raise your voice if you want to be heard! You've got an opinion—let others hear it, no matter how foolish it is!

When we set out to write "Unleash the Whiner Within," the naysayers told us, "Don't do it. These days it's all about demanding your rights and clearly stating your needs in a positive, confident manner." To that we say, waa, waa! You don't have to demand your rights if you've got a whine that could shatter glass.

Deep inside the easygoing you is a cantankerous you yearning to get out. Set it free! Learn the fine art of carping. Find fault with others—complain, criticize, growl, grumble, grouse, bemoan, snap, and kvetch. Be surly to your heart's content. Be cranky, impatient, sulky, and uptight. Let out your inner pout. We realize that for years songs have been holding the Santa threat over your head, predicting dire Christmas consequences should you dare to pout. But what does Santa know? He owns one suit, works one night a year, and has to crawl down people's chimneys to get into their homes. No one even lets him in the front door! Is that someone you want to model your life after?

So come on, let go and finally be the whiner you were meant to be. You can do it!

Factoid
Reading too many positive thoughts can make you very negative.

Just Say No to People-Pleasing

Do you have an addiction? We're not talking about alcohol, drugs, or even chocolate. We're talking about people-pleasing. People-pleasing is an addiction, and in some cases intervention is desperately needed.

It's time to overcome your need to get on the good side of everyone you meet and focus more on pleasing number one—you! *You* are what matters. *You* are who you should be pleasing. *You* are the one you have to see looking back at you in the mirror every day. *You* are the one you can't afford to offend. After all, what would life be like if you suddenly refused to talk to yourself?

"Hey, me, how could you do something so stupid? What were you thinking?"

"I'm not talking to you!"

"What do you mean, you're not talking to me?"

"I'd rather keep better company."

"You can't just send me away. We're inseparable."

"Watch me!"

"I don't like your attitude!"

"I don't like yours!"

"You want to take this outside?"

"Ooh, like I'm really scared! Look, I've seen you fight. You're a wimp!"

"Yeah? Well, you're a loser!"

"Wimp!"

"Loser!"

"Your momma!"

"Your momma too!"

Do you see our point? If you don't start pleasing yourself, you could offend yourself, and things could turn ugly fast.

Before we talk about a cure for this addiction to pleasing others, let's look at some common signs of a people-pleasing personality.

When confronted with a hostile, rude, and angry individual, do you bend over backward to accommodate the person? For example, such an individual may bump into you on a crowded bus and say something like, "Get out of my way, you idiot!" And your response might be, "Oh, I'm so sorry, I appear to have intruded upon your space. By the way, that's a nice haircut you have. It really complements the tattoo on your cheek and your nose ring. Here, as penance for my getting in your way, please take my wallet. I was going to get a new one anyway."

Does any of that sound familiar? Of course it does. That's because people-pleasers rarely confront. They would rather sit on a fire-ant hill than have to face down some rude individual about his or her obnoxious behavior. But surrendering the power to these rude people is the wrong thing to do. You're empowering them and enabling their bad behavior. The worst thing you can do is give them an open invitation to walk all over you.

Instead, the correct response would be to say, "Ooh, look at

Chapter 5

you, Mr. Tattoo Man (or Ms. Tattoo Woman)! I'm so impressed. Impressed that an individual like you, with so little common sense, was able to amass the seventy-five cents in exact change necessary to board this bus." That's how you establish healthy boundaries. (Note: It might be a good idea to first make sure the person isn't armed before making the common-sense comment. And you might want to make sure you know the location of the exit doors before embarking on this confrontation.)

Let's consider another example.

A people-pleaser is in line in the express lane of the supermarket when a harried, rude person cuts in front of him with thirty-seven items and then proceeds to write a check, even though the sign overhead clearly states, "8 items or less" and, "No checks." But the anarchy doesn't end there. This shopper has forgotten his supersaver membership card, so the store can't accept his check without more information and manager approval. He gives his phone number to the clerk, only it's the number for where he lived in 1987, and thus the clerk is unable to accept the check. The clerk begins the agonizingly slow process of rescanning each individual item to void the sale and have the groceries returned to stock.

Then the rude individual discovers five dollars in his pocket, so he insists the clerk wait while he goes to the back of the store, on the far side, to pick up a carton of milk and a loaf of bread.

Not only does the people-pleaser permit the person to hold up the line while these transactions are taking place, but the people-pleaser actually offers to run and get the milk and bread! This is sick.

Instead of allowing oneself to be treated like a doormat, the correct response when a rude individual takes up that much time while everyone else waits is, "Excuse me, Your Self-Centeredness, the rest of us would like to buy our groceries and return to our homes. I think you belong in that line over there. The one with all the nuts, fruitcakes, and Ding Dongs by it."

A third example is a scenario in which a people-pleaser is getting his or her car repaired. The mechanic says the car needs an oil change and new brakes, as well as a new fan belt, muffler, tires, and an engine. The people-pleaser has had no trouble with these parts, as he had most of them replaced only six months ago. But without questioning the mechanic, the people-pleaser allows the repairs, which will bring his bill for what was supposed to be a simple oil change and brakes to $1,298.

In addition, the people-pleaser is too timid to ask the mechanic for a ride home to wait while the repairs are being done. Instead, he walks twelve miles to the fork in the road and another fourteen after that to his house. He doesn't even retrieve his checkbook or cell phone from the car before leaving (for fear of offending the mechanic, lest he feel the slightest twinge of mistrust from his customer). Later, when he discovers that the mechanic used one of said checks to pay his overdue utility bill and then made three lengthy calls to London from the cell phone, all the people-pleaser can think of to say is, "Did you get a clear connection?"

The correct response, of course, would have been, "Yeah, sure, go ahead and 'fix' those things. And while you're working, I'm just going to excuse myself and call the Better Business Bureau and the Chamber of Commerce to report you for theft of services—and that's only the beginning! What's that? You say you'll change the oil and fix my brakes for free? What a nice person you are!"

Chapter 5

You see? It's simple. With practice, you can quit being stepped on and learn to stand up for yourself. The authors of this book used to be people-pleasers, but we started standing up for ourselves, and look at us now. We don't even let our editor push us around anymo—Hey, what happened? The lights just went out! Hey, come on . . . We were just kidding! Come on . . . we've got a deadline to meet! You can't treat us like this! We're book authors! We deserve better th—

The Complete Moron's Guide to Winning through Hypnosis and Halitosis

There are many ways of achieving your dreams in life. Hard work, persistence, family connections, networking, getting a great education, and waiting until a rich relative dies so you can inherit a large sum of cash are all possibilities.

But forget all that. Those paths to success are nice for people who have four, five, maybe even twenty years to achieve success. For the rest of us, there is the easier way: winning through hypnosis and halitosis.

Winning through Hypnosis and Halitosis is a practical mind-control guide for people who desire to persuade others to give them what they want. For example, say you're at a Starbucks, but the line is long and you don't have time to wait. So what do you do? You tap the person in front of you on the shoulder and blow a big, deep, garlic-filled breath on her. Then take a gold pendant (or an oatmeal cookie) and swing it in front of her eyes while chanting, "Watch the swinging orb . . . see it go back and forth . . . back and forth . . ."

Soon this person will be fully hypnotized. (The garlic breath makes a person dizzy and lowers resistance to the hypnosis.) Now the person is at your beck and call to do whatever you ask. But you don't simply ask. You order! "Get out of line! Get out of line at once!" And, of course, the hypnotized person complies and gets out of line, making the line that much shorter.

Or say you apply for a job, but you don't come close to meeting the qualifications. During the interview you simply breathe on the interviewer and then pull out your little gold orb and swing it back and forth, back and forth . . . "Yes, watch the swinging orb . . . you are in the presence of greatness. This person is the best employee in the world! Offer him the job. Good. Now, don't stop there . . . offer him the corner office. Good . . . now stand on your head and squawk like a chicken. Excellent!"

These are only some of the applications for "Winning through Hypnosis and Halitosis." This method can also have more personal uses.

Say you meet your future in-laws for the first time. But your future mother-in-law just doesn't seem to fancy you. Between the salad and the meat loaf, you grab her and say, exhaling a heavy garlic scent, "Watch the swinging orb! Watch . . ."

Then you breathe on her again. (Mothers-in-law often require an extra dose of garlic breath.) Next, say, "You are in the presence of the greatest son-in-law in history! Offer him your wholehearted approval. And your big-screen TV. Insist that he sit in your husband's chair. Your husband can sit in the folding chair in the corner . . . Excellent! And this Christmas, your wonderful son-in-law isn't going to be sitting at the kiddie table, is he?"

The possibilities are endless. As you can clearly see, "Winning through Hypnosis and Halitosis" is the most powerful and practical course on the market today for attaining your goals. If you don't believe that, watch the swinging golden orb . . .

Maybe People
Just Aren't That
Into You

Bullies, Pests, and Annoying People

The best way to deal with bullies is to stand right up to them.

And then run!

Run like the wind. Turn tail and scram. Cower behind a fire hydrant, a phone booth, a tree, or a mail carrier. This is no time for heroics! Get as far away from the bully as possible.

Sure, many self-help books may advise you differently. They'll say you should stand up to a bully. They'll challenge your manhood or womanhood. They'll chide you for being a wimp. They'll tell you that you have to let the bully know he or she has crossed your boundary. But it's easy for the authors of these books to say that—they're safe and secure hiding behind their publisher's mailing address. They're not in your shoes. They don't have to face your particular bully. They've never felt the fear that courses through your veins every time this person looks in your direction.

We, on the other hand, will counsel you honestly. We say the next time your bully bullies you, don't be a fool. Take off and get as far away as possible. There's no shame in being a chicken. Especially a live one.

However, if you insist on dealing with your bully mano a mano (or a womano a womano), then the least we can do is provide you with some tips.

Tip #1

When facing a bully, it's important to approach with an understanding attitude. Ask your bully why he or she feels the need to bully. Primarily, bullies bully because they feel something is missing from their lives. That missing piece is someone to pick on, and for whatever reason, they think you're the one to fill the bill. In their eyes, you are their personal doormat. They just figure you're fulfilling your purpose in life.

So tell them they're wrong. Put it in a letter and mail it to them when you're safely several hundred miles away.

Tip #2

Another way to face down bullies is by telephone. Pick up the phone, dial the number, and when they answer, tell them you're tired of being their verbal punching bag. You've had it, and you're not going to take it anymore! Rant that they're so beneath you that they don't even deserve a phone call, but because you're classier than they could ever be, you're bestowing on them this favor.

Then hang up on the time and weather recording, and call your bully and wish him or her a nice day.

Tip #3

A third option for handling bullies is acting as their friend. Invite them to the zoo (then trick them into getting into one of the cages, and lock the gate behind them). Or give them a free trip (a one-way ticket to the destination of their choice). Or send them a box of chocolates (see if Ex-Lax is making truffles now); sometimes a thoughtful gift can turn a bully into milk toast.

Though these tips offer a few creative options, the safest course of action, clearly, is to avoid confronting the bully altogether. After all, is life really so bad as a doormat? You get to be in the great outdoors, and you're the first one to know when company's coming.

Factoid
Self-help book authors are as common as cockroaches—only some are not as attractive.

How to Tell If Someone Is Lying to You

Honesty is the best policy—we all know that. It's wrong to tell a lie. But it's a sad fact of life that occasionally we encounter nefarious individuals who tell us white (or not-so-white) lies in order to manipulate us. It is, therefore, to one's advantage to be able to recognize the subtle signs that a person may be fibbing. If you can recognize a lie, you can immediately call the other person on the falsehood—or choose not to say a word, but at least you'll know you're being misled. Being able to recognize when someone is not being forthright will give you a huge advantage in life.

So let's examine some of the tip-offs that someone might be lying to you.

Shifting Eyes

When the person speaking to you shifts her eyes back and forth faster than a car at the Indianapolis 500, there's an excellent chance you're not getting the truth, the whole truth, and nothing but the truth. If she's asleep, however, and you can't see her eyes, but she's muttering something about meeting a guy named Luther for lunch tomorrow at a local deli, you might want to listen closely and be at the deli eating your own corned-beef sandwich at noon.

Crossed Fingers

When you notice the speaker has both hands behind his back, with his fingers crossed, this is a sure sign you're not getting the straight skippy. If he's barefoot or wearing sandals, check to see if his toes are crossed too. (If he's not barefoot or wearing sandals, subtly ask him to remove his shoes.) Crossed fingers and toes could signal either a lie or severe muscle cramping. You'll need to determine which it is before launching accusations and causing a scene.

Muttering

And then she said, mutter, mutter...

When the speaker makes a statement and then suddenly mutters, "I hope I don't get caught in this lie!" it is frequently a sign you're being played.

Shifting Balance

When the speaker rocks from side to side until she's eventually speaking while standing on one foot, you may not be hearing the gospel truth.

Perspiration

When the speaker is perspiring so heavily that there's a pool at his feet the size of Lake Superior, better be careful: you may be hearing an untruth.

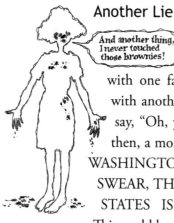

Another Lie

And another thing, I never touched those brownies!

Frequently those who stretch the truth won't be content with one falsehood but will follow that up with another lie. For example, a person may say, "Oh, yes, I got the raise I asked for"— then, a moment later, shout out, "GEORGE WASHINGTON WAS RUSSIAN!" or, "I SWEAR, THE CAPITAL OF THE UNITED STATES IS TALLAHASSEE, FLORIDA!" This could be a subtle indication she may not be the most honest person around.

Hair Pulling

The speaker makes a statement ("I own a brand-new BMW"), then begins violently pulling out large clumps of hair from his own head. This could be a sign he's misleading you.

Chapter 6

Blurting

When the person you're listening to suddenly blurts out a statement like, "Boy, am I glad I'm not hooked up to a lie detector right now," this may be an inadvertent revelation that she hasn't been entirely honest.

Blushing

When the face of the person you suspect of lying turns such a bright shade of red that you need UV-protection sunglasses to look at him, some intentional misdirection may be at work.

Nose Growing

If the speaker's nose suddenly grows two inches, take heed: there could be trouble in River City.

Words Not Matching Actions

When a person nervously fidgets with her new diamond necklace, diamond bracelet, and diamond earrings while asking you for a loan, it could mean she's misrepresenting her financial standing just a tad.

Backpedaling

When a person backs up on his stories so many times he should be equipped with a beeping device like a garbage truck, he just might be spreading some of his own garbage.

Too Good to Be True

When what a person says is too good to be true, it probably is. For example: "I will paint and reroof your home for $246, but it all has to be paid up front. In cash. Gold fillings, with or without the tooth, accepted."

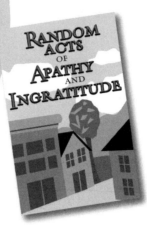

Random Acts of Apathy and Ingratitude

The following acts of apathy are being randomly featured here for your reading enjoyment:

1. A man was sitting on the ground beside a busy highway. He was unable to walk anywhere in style, as he owned no designer shoes. Then one day a truck from a well-known discount shoe store went past, and a pair of brand-new shoes was tossed to the man. After examining the quality of the shoes, the man tossed them aside and elected to spend the rest of his life sitting beside the busy highway. He did not own a pair of designer shoes, and he did not care.

2. A woman moved to a new city, where she didn't know a single person. She was completely alone, but she purchased a phone and answering machine nonetheless. The phone never, ever rang. Then one day the woman returned home and found a ten-minute recorded message from a complete stranger. He said she sounded so sad

on the answering machine that he wondered if there was anything he could do to help cheer her. Were the story to end here, this would be a touching, feel-good tale. Unfortunately, the woman sued the man for violating antistalking laws.

3. A man was driving down the road a few days before Christmas in a cold Midwestern town. He happened upon a man whose car had broken down. The hood was up, and the man leaned over his stalled engine, shivering in the icy wind.

   The man who was driving pulled over and told the stranded man he should call a motor club for assistance. When the man with the stalled car replied that he was not a member, the other man said, "Oh," and drove off.

Penmanship Analysis

Some self-help books will lead you to believe that you can tell a lot about a person by analyzing his or her handwriting. We don't believe in that. However, analyzing the person's penmanship is another thing altogether.

Penmanship can give insight into a person's character, morality, ambition, and of course, motor skills. We've often said that employers should abstain from even glancing at a prospective employee's resume or references and should instead examine the applicant's penmanship when determining whether to offer him or her a job.

Potential spouses should certainly consider their beloved's background, data collected by private investigators, and clothing choices; but they should not overlook the wealth of information available only by close examination of the betrothed's cursive skills. Choosing the person you want to spend the rest of your life with isn't a decision you should arrive at willy-nilly.

We've included here several penmanship examples to demonstrate the value of penmanship analysis.

It's easy to see that this sample reveals an oversized ego. The writer believes he has a mandate to get what he wants and feels others should be at his beck and call. The best professional roles for this person include politician, used-car salesperson, sports agent, and auto mechanic.

I'm not here.

This person has the self-esteem of a fruit fly. She believes she's insignificant and therefore is easily walked on. She takes other people's guff without question. Such an individual is easily manipulated, so some good career choices might include assistant to a temporary personal assistant, retail store clerk, nursery worker, and comedy writer.

☺☺☺☺ ☺☺ ☺ ☺ ☺☺☺☺☺☺
You're OK, I'm delirious.

This penmanship sample hints at an individual who is overly optimistic. She tends to see the world through rose-tinted glasses. She buys twenty bingo cards every week because she's certain she'll win this time. When the doorbell rings, this person rushes to the door in anticipation of seeing the Publisher's Clearing House Prize Patrol. Such an individual can be nauseatingly upbeat, even telling her mugger to have a nice day or, worse yet, writing him a check because she doesn't have enough cash on hand to make it worth his while. Potential career paths include entertainment reporter, greeter at Baskin-Robbins, and flight attendant.

☹☹☹☹☹☹☹☹☹☹☹ ☹☹☹☹☹☹☹☹
Have whatever kind of day you want. What do I care?

Conversely, this sample indicates that the writer is overly pessimistic. Potential careers for this person might include chairman of the Federal Reserve or vice president of the United States.

This type of handwriting reveals an individual with arrested development. That is, if the writer is an adult. If this sample is from a four-year-old, then this is normal. Most likely career paths would be doctor or pharmacist.

Maybe Life's Just Not That Into You

Chapter 7

How to Succeed and Be Happy in Business without Doing Anything Sensible!

Self-improvement books offer a unique (some might say skewed) idea of what a person must do to succeed and be happy. Some authors may even be opposed to traditional therapists, educators, counselors, ministers, and other professionals, taking a decidedly different view of what it takes to make it in life.*

Let's take a look at some of the ideas traditionalists cling to as compared with what many self-help authors advocate as the way to get ahead in life.

Traditonalists	Many Self-Help Authors
Advocate education and learning in order to make informed decisions.	Make decisions based on the position of certain stars . . . and their book's standing on the *New York Times* bestseller list.
Believe the way to earn respect is to earn an advanced degree.	Believe the way to earn respect is to arbitrarily place letters after your name. PhD? Sure! Does anyone really check those things anyway?
Prepare for difficult times by establishing a firm foundation with a strong nuclear family at its core.	Prepare for difficult times by walking on hot coals.
Recommend eating a well-balanced diet.	Promote the consumption of nothing but water (preferably cherry flavored) for nine days straight.
A likely mantra: "Life is what you make of it."	A likely mantra: "Send $29.99 to join my Web community."
Both sexes are created equal.	Men are scum.
A penny saved is a penny earned.	The Lazy Dude's Guide to Riches
There are no shortcuts in life.	Thin Thighs in 30 Days
Suggests beginning each day with a healthy breakfast.	Suggests beginning each day by chanting one thousand affirmations about why you're no longer a loser. And a bowl of oatmeal.
Advocates belief in a higher power.	Advocates belief in a Swami named Ed.

* It's important to note that these self-help authors are not in sync with the mainstream, and the "easily swayed" may be in danger of having their lives turned upside down (and be out $29.99) by overenthusiastic, underqualified self-help gurus.

The Traveler's Gift Exchange

The following is a nearly true story, told to us by someone who overheard a taxi driver telling his dispatcher this story. We tracked down the uncle of the dispatcher, and here is the story in the very words he heard. Or most of them.

After a freak airport accident in which I collapsed onto the baggage carousel at LAX and made twelve trips around before a man finally noticed my predicament and called for help (apparently I had fallen onto his suitcase and he was having trouble getting it out from under me), I had an out-of-body experience. While I was in that unconscious state, I went on a journey in my mind and was met by a handful of historical figures who taught me the seven great lessons of life.

I met former president Richard M. Nixon, who took me aside into a little corner office. I noticed he had not shaved in some time, he had a heavy five-o'clock shadow. He paced throughout the office, stopping to chat with paintings of other historical figures on the wall. I wondered why, but I didn't question.

When Mr. Nixon finally turned back and gave me his undivided attention, he relayed to me one of the great "Decisions for Success." He told me, "As you walk through life, remember: always erase all of your audiotapes—taking out a portion simply won't do."

I also met others on my journey. Their names escape me at the moment, but the important lessons they taught me on my journey will be forever etched in my memory. These are what these other travelers taught me.

1. The buck starts here

Have you noticed that few people take personal responsibility these days? They blame their mistakes on others. They pass the buck and backpedal and rewrite history and make excuses and skirt the issues and shift the blame to everyone but themselves. And now you can too! Why be the only one standing up and taking responsibility for your own stupid mistakes? Why have the buck stop when you can watch it go sailing off into the sunset, as far away from you as possible? Why, it might even make it all the way around the world before it ever comes back to you!

2. Seek dumb and untested advice

Forget about getting wise counsel. What you need are the opinions of losers. Who better to give you financial advice than someone from Wall Street? No, not someone from a Wall Street institution—we're talking about that ex-broker with the shopping cart who's sitting in front of the Stock Exchange playing the ukulele. Now there's someone whose advice is worth listening to. After all, if you can't learn from those who have squandered their wealth and opportunities through poor life choices, risky financial maneuverings, and seedy associations, who can you learn from?

3. Be a person of inaction

Anyone can be a courageous leader. But courageous leaders sometimes get killed. Why put your body through that uncomfortable process? It can hurt. Really hurt. So do the thing courageous leaders wish they could do but are simply too afraid to try: hide! They can't ask you to lead anybody anywhere if they can't find you!

4. Double your pleasure, double your mind

We ask you, what has single-mindedness done for anyone? Sure, it can make you appear more focused and alert, but how boring is that?

If you can walk and chew gum at the same time, just think how many other things you could do simultaneously. Conflicting goals, contrasting ideas, and double bookings in your day planner are just some of the things you can juggle once you start dividing your attention. Life in a constant state of confusion and chaos isn't as bad as you might think.

5. Choose grumpiness

Grumpiness doesn't just happen. You have to pursue it. You have to work at it. You have to be constantly honing your grumpitude. But the results are well worth it. It's even been shown that grumpiness can prolong your life. (Rumor has it that Grumpy outlived all the other dwarfs by 140 years.) It makes sense. Grumpiness keeps people away from you, and people have germs. If germs can't get near you, you won't catch things like colds, the flu, or the bubonic plague. Before you know it, you'll have reached a ripe old grumpy age and could be enjoying the admiration of all your friends . . . if you had any.

6. Forget pumping iron. For real muscle growth, hold grudges.

Sure, we all need grace and mercy. But it's a lot more fun to hold grudges, be self-righteous, and keep all the grace and mercy to yourself, isn't it? And you should see the muscles you'll grow just hauling an old grudge around with you.

7. Persevere by bullying others until the end

We've already talked about bullies, yet it bears repeating. Being bullied is no fun. But bullying? Well, that's a different story altogether. If you can be the one to do the bullying first, chances are good you won't have to worry about ever being bullied again.

Finding True Happiness

What is happiness? Good question. Contrary to what some believe, true happiness isn't found on a well-stocked dessert tray (that is abounding joy, not happiness). Neither is happiness found in a Super Bowl win for your favorite team. (That's sheer ecstasy, not happiness.)

Happiness is that elusive something we all want. Some of us spend our lives in pursuit of happiness. The U.S. Constitution affirms that as our God-given right. But the mere pursuit of happiness doesn't mean we'll ever truly attain it. Like a butterfly fluttering freely in front of us, we may never fully fathom its freedom nor tame its flittering flight. To which you may be inclined to say, "What?!"

Exactly.

And therein lies the mystery. Why do some people simply sit back, relax, and allow happiness to fly to them while others sit back and watch happiness flutter away? And where do kazoos fit into the scheme of things? Let's explore.

146

The key—the well-kept secret—to finding true happiness is twofold: (1) we must think happy thoughts, and (2) we must force all the negative, unhappy thoughts out of our heads. That's all there is to it!

During our research at the Happiness Institute, we have perfected a number of tried-and-true thoughts that we recommend cultivating if you desire true happiness. And we've also developed a list of thoughts to avoid at all cost if you don't want to be a victim of unhappiness. It's all a matter of keeping your mind on good thoughts and off of the bad thoughts.

Happy Thoughts

- Balloons

- Stuffed animals (unless you had yours ripped from your arms by a bully in your first-grade class and have nightmares about it to this day)

- Chocolate milk shakes

- Puppies

- Lazy Sundays

- Rainbows

- Shiny new cars

- Waterfalls (unless you had a near-drowning experience one summer while whitewater rafting at the camp your parents sent you to)

- Kazoos

Chapter 7

- Clowns (unless one tried to run over you with his little clown car)
- Fat royalty checks from your new self-help book

Unhappy Thoughts

- Taxes
- Death
- Sickness
- The national debt
- Mice running loose in your house
- Yard work
- Having a seat in an airplane next to someone with the flu
- Global warming
- Having a seat in an airplane next to a screaming kid
- Traffic jams
- Having a seat in an airplane next to a guy who looks eerily like the man you saw featured on *America's Most Wanted*
- Blind dates
- Having a seat on an airplane between a guy who looks eerily like the man you saw featured on *America's Most Wanted* and his screaming kid with the flu

Awaken the Behemoth Within

Let's hear from one of the better-known motivational speakers on the circuit today. No, not Tony Robbins. Tony Robbings. No relation. Our Tony says:

A couple of years ago, I had it quite rough. I was working twelve hours a day as a janitor at a sewage plant built next to a leaking nuclear facility and across from a dollar store that even the rats avoided. In my spare time I practiced walking barefoot on hot coals to round out my preparation for my future career as a giant who gives advice to others and walks on hot coals.

After my twelve-hour shift as a janitor at the sewage plant, I had to walk twenty-seven miles home to my one-room efficiency apartment that was too tiny to accommodate my six-foot seven-inch height. At night I slept with my legs stuck out into the corridor. The other apartment-building residents frequently tripped over me as they left for work in the morning. It was a horrible existence. But I stayed

Chapter 7

focused on my future and one day was finally able to raise myself out of this dismal existence.

How? I'll tell you how: by coming up with a belief system! And you can do it too! If you want to succeed, know what you believe and then believe what you believe and do what you believe; but believe me, the most important thing of all is to believe what you believe!

I believe that I can be whatever I set my mind to. Except maybe a camel. Although I haven't tried.

In addition to a belief system, you'll need a game plan and a mentor. I see so many people walking around who don't have a plan or a mentor or belief in themselves— people who probably have never ever walked barefoot on a single hot coal. I feel so sorry for them, those poor, deprived individuals.

I remember back when I was a small boy and my best friend's mother was a kind, rather large woman who had no beliefs or mentors and who never, ever walked on hot coals. She had barbequed plenty of ribs on them, but she'd never walked on them. And she seemed sad. I wanted to help, but back then I didn't have any DVDs, books, or even a VHS tape series to sell her, so I couldn't do anything to lighten her heavy load. Today, as far as I know, she still hasn't walked on any coals. How sad.

I had another friend whose mother drank too much; she was impossible to deal with. Until one day she began setting goals and writing those goals down on a piece of paper. After several months of writing down each and every goal she set for herself, she began finding purpose and meaning in her life—and walking on hot coals! Her feet have third-degree burns, and she's lost two toes due to skin grafts gone awry, but she has her mind set on her goals, and nothing can deter her!

With a system of ironclad goals, anyone can emerge from a going-nowhere life and find true happiness. Life is all about a system of beliefs and plans—planning your system and believing in your system and in your beliefs and in your plan, or plans and beliefs. This is what it's all about, friends, plans and beliefs. And of course, hot coals.

It's Important to Have Good Role Models

"One small step for man, one giant leap for mankind."
—Neil Armstrong

"Ouch, oh! Ow—ohhhh!"
—Me, walking on hot coals

Three Super-Duper Secrets to a Peaceful Existence

Secret 1: Keep an open mind

We all were raised with a certain value system, with basic beliefs, and were taught certain lessons. Just for fun, let your mind flow freely, and let go of that value system. Not forever—just for now. Just for these few moments. Let it all evaporate, freeing your mind for something truly enlightening, like thinking about that Snickers bar in your pocket.

After you've let go of your value system—all the norms and standards and everything you were raised to believe—imagine this: A frog is president of the United States. He has a cabinet of tadpoles, and the First Lady is a toad. This team of frogs runs the country. Isn't it enlightening? Imagine . . . a nation run by frogs!

Now go back to your value system. What were you thinking? You need a value system—do you want the whole world to fall apart?!

Secret 2: Silence is wonderful

Do you hear it? Do you know what that is? It's silence. In our society, where we're bombarded with noise and confronted with a constant cacophony of sound, isn't it peaceful to hear . . . nothing?

Every day the average person has sixty thousand thoughts. (People who work at the DMV have four.) Isn't it fun to just let your mind go blank and listen to the silence? It really is true: silence is golden. So are the arches. Are you feeling hungry?

153

Secret 3: Drawing large flowers on every page takes up space, and we don't have to write as much

Did you ever notice that? Did you think we put these flowers on every page to establish a calm, relaxing vibe? Well, yes, that's a small part of it—but mostly the flowers just reduce the amount of work for us. So sit back and enjoy. They're nice flowers, aren't they? Nice, peaceful flowers. Say, "I am at peace." Say it again. Louder. Louder still.

"Hey, what are you doing?! We told you to be silent!"

Think Small . . . A Collector's Edition

Not being effective is really ineffective.

You want joy? Then find joy.

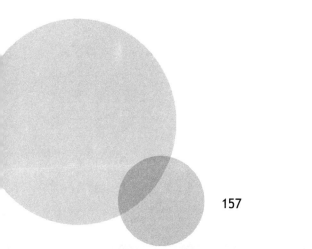

157

Scratch that itch; it's yours to scratch.

Fluffy clouds are the best clouds.

I like to say silly things. That's part of being free, Sasquatch.

Want to have some fun tomorrow?

Call all your friends and family
and announce that you're
changing your name to Purdue.

It's easier to be happy than to feel silly.

162

Isn't white space on a page beautiful?

Just for fun,

    right now,

        stop what you're doing

            and wiggle your nose.

        Isn't that a hoot?

Want to feel happy?

Imagine you've just written a best-selling book
that contains about ninety words!

Too Soon Smart,
Too Late Old...

No Wait...It's

"Too Soon Wise,
Too Late Stu—"

❦

Nevermind.

Too Soon Smart, Too Late Old . . .

But since we brought it up, here are . . .

10 True Things You Really Need to Know

1. If a man finds an acorn, it may turn out to be something other than an acorn—say, perhaps, a toothbrush.

   Meaning: Things aren't always the way they seem, particularly if you've lost your glasses.

2. A magician pulls a rabbit from a hat, but never from a ball cap.

   Meaning: Success in life can only be accomplished when one uses the proper tools.

3. Birds go south for the winter; retirees go south for good.

   Meaning: Self-explanatory.

4. Laughter is the gravy on life's mashed potatoes.

   Meaning: The addition of laughter to one's life, much like

*the addition of gravy to a fine potato, makes things better.
A stick of butter can also significantly improve a potato,
but adding a stick of butter to one's life rarely makes a large
difference, and on a hot summer day it can make your car
seats slippery.*

5. Bad things sometimes happen to those who sing a
   cappella in high heels.

   Meaning: Even we have no idea what this one means.

6. Life is like a lottery, the major difference being you don't
   have to buy tickets at a convenience store to participate
   in life.

   Meaning: Life is a gamble, but no "scratchers" are required.

7. To some species a female sea cow is more attractive than a
   supermodel.

   Meaning: Beauty is in the eye of the beholder.

8. A red necktie is not always a sign of power.

   *Meaning: This is especially true when the wearer of the red
   necktie is being chased up a tree by a bull.*

9. A banana has a peel, and unpeeling a banana sometimes
   reveals a piece of fruit that is unripe.

   *Meaning: Sometimes those who are green are thrust into the
   limelight before their time.*

10. Tuup frtg byoutre reto byerto hyuoe.

    *Meaning: Hey, it makes as much sense as anything else on
    this list.*

Nothing but Questions

Because we know you're tired of people offering you practical help and giving you all the answers, we present the following section of "Nothing but Questions." Answer these to get to know yourself a little better.

- If you could be any celebrity's belt, whose would you be?

- If you discovered a new planet, what would you name it—and what do you have against naming it Ralph?

- Which letter do you like better: C or H? And why are you thinking of sugar right now?

- If you could paint a frog pink or magenta, which color would you choose?

- If you had three hands, what's the first thing you'd do with the third one?

- If you were an ant, would you choose to be a queen or a worker?

- If you were a member of Britain's royal family, what kind of embarrassing scandal would you be involved in?

- Which do you like better: your nose or your ears?

- If you could give a wedgie to any famous historical figure, who would it be?

Factoid
Some self-help books are to serious literature what William Hung is to classical music.

Being Your Very, Very, Best Friend

It's a myth that you need others to validate your feelings and serve as sounding boards. You can be your own best friend by simply exploring the difference between how you feel and what is objectively true.

Feeling: I feel like I am alone in the world—all the time.

Truth: You are not alone in the world; you are constantly surrounded by those who care for you and visit regularly. Just think, there's the mail carrier, the meter reader, perhaps the newspaper delivery person, and all those nice magazine salespeople who ring your doorbell just as you're about to step into the shower.

Feeling: I often feel no one is listening.

Truth: . . . What?

Feeling: It's impossible for me to have a happy life. I had a miserable childhood and now suffer from low self-esteem.

Truth: Don't be ridiculous! Don't let the fact that you're an annoying twit with too much time on your hands hold you back!

Feeling: I'm trying to be my own best friend, but what's the point?

Truth: Can you say carpool lane?

Feeling: People never seem to have time for me.

Truth: I'll get back to you right after the game.

Feeling: Hey, what kind of self-improvement book is this, anyway?

Truth: Wait a minute . . . Touchdown! . . . OK, back to you. Really, you need to get a life and stop asking stupid questions.

Chicken Cacciatore for the Complete Moron's Soul

It's finally here! The book that combines two of the most popular series in history—the "for Morons" manuals and the Chicken Cacciatore for the Soul books—into one smashing title, Chicken Cacciatore for the Complete Moron's Soul.

The following is a sample true story. Only the people and facts have been made up. Any animal mentioned is real, however, and thus they shall remain anonymous.

Back in the day, I used to walk five miles to the general store. It was a long walk up a hilly gravel road used mostly by folks looking for a shortcut or an alternative to the interstate. On one journey, halfway to my destination, I encountered him. Looking slightly ragged and with a pronounced bald spot half the size of Montana, he was standing beside the road.

I immediately noticed he was carrying "it" under his arm—one of those ubiquitous "for Morons" manuals I always see in bookstores but never read. I believe this one was Auto Repair for Morons, or something like that. I stopped and said hello. The man said hello and offered to share with me what he had just gleaned from his book.

The next hour was spent in joyous rapture at the wealth of knowledge found in said tome. It covered everything from what a spark plug looks like to where the gas cap goes while not in use (on top of the roof) to where the backseat is located (usually behind the front seat) to what to do if you have a flat tire (sell the car).

I eventually thanked the moron for sharing this store of information and continued on my journey (thanks to the Atlas for Morons the man had given me).

Several days later I was traveling the same gravel road and again came upon the moron. This time he had a different book under his arm: Home Maintenance for Morons. I sat in stony silence as he regaled me with all the hidden treasures in this volume: how to remove a plug from a light socket (not while standing in water), how to pound a nail (preferably with a hammer), what to do if there's an electrical fire (get out the wieners), and who to call if you're unable to complete roof maintenance yourself (a duct-tape factory).

After listening to the moron for over two hours, I left with the impression that this was perhaps the wisest man in the entire county, if not the world.

I didn't see the moron on my next several walks to the general store, and I began to fear he had taken ill or had been arrested for vagrancy, or that he'd been eaten by a wild animal.

I later learned from friends who worked at the general store that the moron had indeed taken ill and was hospitalized. I climbed into my car and drove the eight miles to the nearest hospital, St. Ann's, and found the moron. He was all alone in his room, with no visitors, just as I suspected.

The moron nodded to me in greeting. In his hands was the book *Health Tips for Complete Morons*. He told me that he had scheduled himself for surgery the following morning and asked if I thought I could assist. He handed me a book called *Appendectomies for Complete Morons*. It looked pretty self-explanatory, so I agreed to help.

Things didn't go very well during the operation (apparently there was a typo in the book), but luckily, he also had the books *Funerals for Complete Morons* and *110 Ways to Prepare Chicken Cacciatore*, so I was prepared for whatever might happen. And I felt at peace.

How to Find Love, Lose Weight, Defeat Anger, Get Rich, Get Even, and Build Six-Pack Abs in 30 Days or Less

The clock is ticking! We have just thirty days in which to help you find love, lose weight, defeat anger, get rich, get even, and most importantly, build six-pack abs. So get moving! It's time for action. On your mark, get set, let's go!

First let's go looking for love. True love. Not that puppy kind of love. Meaningful love, in which you meet, go on a few dates, and get to the altar in less than a month. Love that gets you out of waiting until the next family wedding to meet that girl your Uncle Henry has been wanting to set you up with. Love that means no waiting for your next high-school reunion so you can finally ask out the cheerleader you've had a crush on since 1962—the one who never married but still has that youthful look (with pimples and braces). Real love, that's what we're talking about.

The best way to find love in thirty days or less is to quit being so ridiculously picky. Sure, the girl might have a horse laugh, but have you listened to some of your own noises lately? That thing you do with your adenoids can be pretty irritating. And look—those love handles on your sides are getting big enough to set a lamp on. Finding true love in thirty days or less is going to be difficult enough without your demanding that the girl of your dreams have a full set of teeth. But by giving up unreasonable desires like that, you'll not only find yourself saying, "I do"—you'll also save a fortune on dental bills.

So the next time you're at a party or some other function where there are more occupants in the room than you and your dog, remember: be flexible. Don't disqualify every member of the opposite sex by being too picky. The love of your life could be just one toothless hello away. But the clock is ticking!

Now on to weight loss. How does one lose a significant amount of weight in thirty days or less? Easy. Exercise without the brownies in each hand.

Next topic: how to defeat anger. Simply get your brownies back!

And what about getting rich in thirty days or less? This is easy too. Do you have any idea how many wishing wells there are in this country? (All right, we're just kidding. Other than for supplementing your retirement income, we would never advocate your diving into a wishing well and scooping up the hundreds, perhaps thousands of dollars in loose change just lying there in full view—and reach—of passersby. That would be wrong. Besides, you could drown going down for a quarter. Is it really worth it?) No, no. Get rich the old-fashioned way: marry a millionaire!

On to how to get even in thirty days or less: get an enemy's son or daughter to marry you.

And finally, how do you build six-pack abs in thirty days or less? Immediately after reading this paragraph, take this book and wedge it under your feet. Then place your hands behind your head and perform ten sit-ups.

Go on. We'll wait . . .

Done? OK, feel your stomach. Do you feel anything at all that feels like a six-pack? Like maybe that six-pack of soda you just strapped around your waist? Great! Now you've got six-pack abs!

So there you have it. Your first steps toward a new you. Just follow these simple rules for another twenty-nine days and you will have gained love, lost weight, defeated anger, increased your wealth, gotten even, and developed six-pack abs. See how easy that was? And you didn't even have to risk wishing-well diving to do it!

DON'T SWEAT
THE TINY STUFF.
sure, lose a little sleep,
maybe chew your nails a bit,
but don't sweat

Guidlines to Make Room
for the Bigger Challenges
in Your Life

Don't Sweat the Tiny Stuff

If we were honest with ourselves, most of us would agree that it's the tiny stuff that gets us down. That fish bone we're choking on, the splinter in our thumb that's causing it to get infected and swell to twice its normal size, the tack we sat on, the shard of glass we stepped on . . . Tiny things can ruin our day.

But they don't have to! All we have to do is focus on the larger things in life and forget all about the tiny stuff. Large things like that eighteen-wheeler that has crossed over into our lane and is heading right at us, or the elephant that got loose at the circus and is trampling everyone in the stands around us, or the meteor shower that's on track to crash down on our house (the den, to be exact).

But that's all right. If we don't sweat the tiny stuff, we'll have the energy we need to handle the larger things and to do what we should be doing all along: having a love affair with life. All of life. Every day, it's important to fall in love with life—the trees, the grass, the sky, the oceans, Graham crackers, shoehorns, porcupines, radishes, beach balls—just drink up life and swallow it whole. And if and when that meteor shower does come, just remember to stay out of the den, and duck!

Maybe Self-Help Authorship *Is* Into You!

Chapter 8

Maybe Self-Help Authorship Is Into You!

You Might Be a Self-Help Author If . . .

- You include a bogus "PhD" after your name, even though the highest level of education you've had is traffic school (which you flunked out of).

- You grew up in the suburbs of Toledo, yet you insist others call you Swami.

- You think anything can be accomplished in thirty days or less. You don't understand why the Egyptians couldn't have completed the pyramids in less than four weeks. "Couldn't they have just bought a kit?" you ask.

- You refuse to answer any question people ask you that

doesn't begin with, "O great self-help guru of the new millennium."

- Your goals in life are to attain a higher level of spiritual awakening, resulting in total peace and contentment, and to appear on *Oprah* (not necessarily in that order).

- Your wife says that in your sleep you often mumble, "I'm good enough, I'm smart enough, I'm attractive enough . . . now give me more of the blanket!"

- You've completed a 750-page book with barely enough actual information to fill out a pie chart.

- You have a penchant for large print and tiny thoughts.

- On a local TV talk show, you once cut off a Girl Scout's microphone to secure more time for yourself.

- You want to help people and to make a difference, and you feel the best way to accomplish that is by charging $19.95 for access to the material on your Web site.

- You love exclamation marks so much you even include one after your name, as in "Jonas H. Polk, PhD!"

Requirements for Becoming a Self-Help Guru

Writing a self-help book is not for everyone. Only a select few have what it takes to build a successful career penning volumes of advice. So if you've ever dreamed of becoming a self-help author, or "Greed Guru" as some have printed in invisible ink on their business cards, you'll need to meet the following criteria. (Of course, this doesn't apply to all self-help books. Just the kind we like to read.)

- Lack of knowledge in one or more particular fields

- An exaggerated sense of self-worth, leading one to believe he or she is the ultimate authority in one or more areas, frequently including, but not limited to: finding love, recovering from lost love, getting even with last love, depression, anger (how to get angry, how to stop being angry, or how to get angry about being asked about getting angry), dieting, overcoming loss, the art of small talk with strangers, how to ditch those strangers when they turn out to be stalkers, daily affirmations and banal slogans, and how to avoid starchy foods, difficult people, and free advice when so much good advice is available for a mere $69.99 for the entire book and CD collection (also available on cassette tapes)

- A tendency to refer to oneself in the third person: "When Don Chase discovered the cure for plantar warts, Don Chase simply had to tell the world. Who is Don Chase? I'm glad you asked . . ."

- A confusing style of writing, hence the need for the companion book to help readers decipher the hidden code

- A tireless love of relaying "interesting" anecdotes about oneself, especially including . . .

  1. How the author personally overcame poverty (she did without dessert once), shyness (it was so bad she could hardly answer her four cell phones), and an extreme overbite (he once ate a Big Mac and didn't even realize it)

  2. How her "neglectful" family wouldn't loan her money for the hundredth time without receiving so much as a thank-you in return

- A large, omnipresent ego

- An annoying habit of spouting positive affirmations wherever one goes

- An obsessive need to acquire money by selling a truckload of books, tapes, or videos, almost like a street dealer but (in most instances) without the gun

- A love of the limelight and a need to wear way too much makeup on camera

- The ability to sit in front of a computer, make up stuff at will, and call it a book

- A predisposition to include gratuitous, lettered credentials after one's name, as in "Maxwell J. Kierkendall, PhD, DDS, OFM, OVERBEARINGBORE"

10 Affirmations for Self-Help Authors

1. I deserve to raise the price of my newsletter, "Finding Inner Joy and Six-Pack Abs through Self-Tickling," to $9.99 per month.

2. I can write a 130-page tome with only eight hundred words by writing just a few words per page. And including a paper-cut warning to speed readers.

3. The print on the page is so large, astronauts on the International Space Station are able to identify three landmarks—the Rocky Mountains, the Himalayan Mountains, and your type font.

4. By thinking positive thoughts, I have the power to attain the three most important things in life: world peace, good health, and thighs of steel.

5. I only use exclamation marks when they're truly warranted! I mean it!!!

6. I don't fear the audience finding out the truth about my story of an old neighbor who attained happiness through the positive imagery discussed in my book, despite his being born with four ears. (He actually attained it through being a good listener.)

7. I need to work through my own angst, but I need an audience.

8. I want to meet Dr. Laura, and having my book next to hers in the bookstore might be the closest I ever get.

9. I am worthy of immense personal profits, because my only goal is to make the world a better place. For my accountant.

10. I am at peace with myself after refunding about half of the money I made after renaming my Web site Googled.com.

Self-Help
Book Quiz

Chapter 9

Self-Help Book Quiz

Here's a quick test to see what you've learned about some of the self-help books on the market today and some of their authors.

1. The main purpose of some self-help books is . . .
   a. to improve the world.
   b. to improve oneself.
   c. to contribute to society.
   d. to fatten the author's wallet.

2. Some self-help authors are . . .
   a. committed to producing superior work.
   b. socially conscious, moral people.
   c. caring and encouraging.
   d. self-serving, self-focused, self-help-themselves-to-your-wallets zealots who believe they, and they alone, hold the key to success.

3. Some self-improvement books are . . .
   a. Pulitzer Prize winners.
   b. Nobel Prize winners.
   c. best-selling works of literature.
   d. used as doorjambs.

4. Some self-help books should be . . .
   a. placed in a prominent position on one's bookshelf.
   b. read in one sitting.

    c. loaned to friends you care about.

    d. dropped off at the recycling center soon after the reader gets to page five.

5. The major redeeming quality of many self-improvement books is . . .

    a. their ability to inspire.

    b. their contribution to a lively debate.

    c. their thought-provoking advice.

    d. the interesting way they incorporate the $25 price tag into the cover design.

6. Some self-help books . . .

    a. are well written.

    b. are well researched.

    c. are well thought out.

    d. are probably composed in about a day and a half, while the author was watching the Cartoon Network.

7. Some self-improvement authors are best known for their . . .

    a. introspection and self-awareness.

    b. superb writing and people skills.

    c. deft use of the English language.

    d. really bad toupees.

8. Some self-help books can be easily recognized by . . .

    a. their tight, witty writing and challenging affirmations.

    b. their obsessive-compulsive numbering and lettering of every single point.

   c. an excess of exclamation points!!!!!

   d. the author's face on the front cover and every chapter introduction page of the book

9. Some self-improvement books . . .

   a. are long, exhaustive reads, but well worth the time.

   b. are informative and inspiring.

   c. contain as much real information as a bubblegum wrapper.

   d. contain less real information than a bubblegum wrapper.

10. Which of the following sentences sounds like it comes from a self-help book?

   a. "To be or not to be, that is the question."

   b. "Call me Ishmael."

   c. "May the force be with you."

   d. "Frankly, Scarlett, I don't give a codependent second thought about you! You made your bed, now lie in it. I have healthy boundaries now. My self-esteem is back. My life has purpose and meaning. So keep your Tara, your 'boyfriend,' and your endless drama. Just leave me alone and let me live my life. And to think I didn't even win an Oscar for putting up with you!"

Answers: 1-d, 2-d, 3-d, 4-d, 5-d, 6-d, 7-d, 8-d, 9-d, 10-d

Closing Thoughts

Chapter 10

Closing Thoughts

So there you have it. Like many self-help book authors, we probably haven't fixed anything; but hopefully we've helped you feel more comfortable in your own skin. So what if life's just not that into you? You're here, and you're thriving. And you're successful enough to have paid the cover price for this book. (Unless you bought it at the ninety-nine-cent store, in which case you're still successful enough to have almost a buck on you.)

If we've helped you to laugh a little more about some of the crazy things in life, then we've done what we set out to do. If you've gained a little insight and wisdom from reading this book, then we've done more than we set out to do. But that's OK. That's one of the nice side effects of humor—it helps lower our walls and opens our eyes to some of the things we may want to change about ourselves and our world. If we can laugh about a situation, we're halfway to solving it. Because laughter brings with it a sense of, "We're all in this together."

The books we've parodied are some of the best-selling self-help books on the market. They've sold thousands of copies, so their authors must have done something right. But there are others offering advice to basically change every single thing about yourself, then change it all again when the next fad "fix" comes around. And we hope we've made you stop long enough to think twice about that.

The bottom line is, life's too short to spend it chasing after wealth above all else, a faultless mate, the biggest house, the firmest abs, or the thinnest thighs. Too short for spending all our time and energy trying to please the impossible to please, keep up with the Joneses as they work three jobs trying to keep up with us, and lose fifty pounds while still eating anything we want. Life is too short to waste time reciting nonsensical affirmations we don't understand or torturing ourselves with the latest equivalent to the "therapy" of walking on hot coals.

Life is too short to waste a single minute of it unhappy with who you are in spite of the fact that you're a pretty decent human being. None of us has time to go chasing after a plethora of "keys to happiness." Especially when one of the major keys to happiness is contentment. And that includes contentment with ourselves—in other words, liking who we are. Why are we spending so much time "improving" ourselves when we haven't even taken the time to get to know ourselves in the first place? We get discouraged because we feel we're not making progress fast enough or we don't believe we can measure up to the "perfect" people around us—who in reality aren't all that perfect.

So enjoy life, bumps and all—even with flab abs, a savings account that couldn't buy a book of stamps, and encounters with the unconquered bullies of our lives. The best self-help advice we have to offer is this: Life is what it is; deal with it, improve the things you can, and move on. You'll make more mistakes. Learn from them. You'll lose more money. Try to make better decisions next time. Some people in your life will hurt your feelings, walk on you, remind you of your failures, laugh at your shortcomings, make you feel you have no right to breathe the same air as they do, or do any number of unkind things to you. Why? Because they're as flawed as you are—as we all are.

But as the best self-help books will tell you, don't let any of this stop you from being the person God created you to be. You have a purpose for being alive—don't spend so much time trying to meet someone else's standards that you never get around to doing any of the things you were put on this earth to do.

We've both lost money on real-estate investments, dated people who were all wrong for us, and succumbed to the temptation of a Krispy Kreme doughnut on our way home from the gym. We've had to deal with heartless people and have gone on diets only to watch the scale zoom in the wrong direction. We know what you're going through, and we also know it's not easy. But you can do it!

The most important thing we've learned from life, with all its ups and downs, is what we hope we've communicated in this book—that sometimes you've just got to laugh over what life throws your way. Sure, you may get knocked around a bit, but you've just got to get back up on your feet, brush yourself off, and continue on your way. There's nothing wrong with improving yourself a little more each time you get up, but there's plenty wrong with beating yourself up over yesterday's mistakes or cowering at tomorrow's challenges.

George Eliot once said, "To dream of the person you would like to be is to waste the person you are." Or, to put it another way, to dream of the person you would like to be is to waste the person you are!!!!!

Hmm . . . maybe we wrote a self-help book after all. Or, then again, maybe life's just not that into us either.

Soon to Be Released!

Verbal Chocolate to Raise a Woman's Spirit:
112 Stories of Women Triumphing with Truffles

Synopsis

Verbal Chocolate to Raise a Woman's Spirit is a compilation of 112 stories (and 4,683 calories) of women who used their brains, inner strength, intuition, and an occasional chocolate bar (nuts optional) to overcome tremendous odds and reach the pinnacle of life.

Verbal Chocolate inspires good feelings as it relays semi-true and always-entertaining tales of proud, empowered women fighting off alligators in the Everglades, free-falling from airplanes without parachutes, walking three hundred miles through deserts without food or water, and using that sixth sense some women have to achieve greatness.

Verbal Chocolate to Raise a Woman's Spirit will make any female glad she was born a woman. It's an ode to women everywhere. And while the tale of the pioneer woman who

Soon to Be Released!

in 1724 single-handedly wrestled a grizzly bear to the ground using only her legs while carrying her newborn in her one good arm (we're not sure what happened to her other arm, but the bear was smiling) may sound far-fetched, but we assure you, these stories are all at least 33 percent true and have been very nearly documented.

You'll relish these true stories of women overcoming their inner demons. One woman prevailed in battle against a large municipality that wanted to destroy her home by right of eminent domain to make room for a Wienerschnitzel restaurant. This champion stood in front of the bulldozer and held her ground. And a chili-cheese dog in each hand.

Another woman emerged victorious after her husband left her and their fourteen children on Christmas Eve with no presents or food, unless you count half a fruitcake (which would only last them until August 2035).

Other stories include a woman who tap-danced along the Great Wall of China in the name of freedom; one who raised $4 billion at a community bake sale; and a woman who won the Kentucky Derby without a horse!

Verbal Chocolate to Raise a Woman's Spirit will lift the self-esteem of women throughout the nation—and might even change the Kentucky Derby forever!

(*Verbal Chocolate* is the sequel to *A Thousand Little Pieces of Chocolate*, the popular and controversial book whose author eventually disclosed that he hadn't even eaten a single M&M, or even an M, prior to the writing of his memoir. Reserve your copy today. It's sure to be a bestseller!)

Soon to Be Released!

More Self-Improvement Titles Soon to Be Released

- *The Five People You Meet in an Unemployment Line*

- *Finding Your Life's Fulfillment through Dominoes*

- *How to Act Like Donald Trump, Look Like Donald Trump, Be Like Donald Trump* . . . by Donald Trump

- *10,000 Really Stupid Things Women Do to Mess Up Their Checkbooks*

- *Getting Your Dream Home by Hypnotizing the Seller's Realtor*

The Real Scoop

While the parodies in this book are in no way a criticism or endorsement of any particular self-help book, we did want to provide at least a partial list of some of the books from which we received inspiration. We have twisted, skewered, borrowed, and spun our satirical wit and wisdom from the following self-help tomes. Without these books (some of which have undeniably helped many), this book would be a lot shorter.

Chapter 1

All the Rules: Time-Tested Secrets for Capturing the Heart of Mr. Right

Men Are from Mars, Women Are from Venus

What Women Want Men to Know: The Ultimate Book about Love, Sex, and Relationships for You—and the Man You Love

Are You Made for Each Other? The Relationship Quiz Book

He's Just Not That Into You: The No-Excuses Truth to Understanding Guys

Men Are Like Fish: What Every Woman Needs to Know about Catching a Man

What Smart Women Know

Looking for Love in All the Wrong Places

101 Lies Men Tell Women—and Why Women Believe Them

The Fine Art of Small Talk: How to Start a Conversation, Keep It Going, Build Networking Skills—and Leave a Positive Impression!

*Can Your Relationship Be Saved? How to Know Whether to Stay
    or Go*
Divorce for Dummies

Chapter 2

*Penny Pincher's Handbook: Hundreds of Ways to Make, Save
    Money*
*Rich Dad, Poor Dad: What the Rich Teach Their Kids about
    Money—That the Poor and Middle Class Do Not!*
*How I Turned $50 into $5 Million in Country Property—Part
    Time, and How You Can Do the Same*
*The Millionaire Next Door: The Surprising Secrets of America's
    Wealthy*
Compilation of the many "Bubble" real-estate books
How to Retire Early and Live Well with Less Than a Million Dollars
Compilation of the many "Stock Pick" books

Chapter 3

*Life Extension: A Practical Scientific Approach Adding Years to Your
    Life and Life to Your Years*
The Ultimate Weight Solution: The 7 Keys to Weight Loss Freedom
The Joy of Weight Loss: A Spiritual Guide to Easy Fitness
Dr. Atkins' Diet Revolution
French Women Don't Get Fat: The Secret of Eating for Pleasure
Celebrity Slimming Secrets
The New Detox Diet: The Complete Guide for Lifelong Vitality
*The Abs Diet: The Six-Week Plan to Flatten Your Stomach and Keep
    You Lean for Life*
Compilation of the many "Celebrity Workout" books
Natural Cures "They" Don't Want You to Know About

Chapter 4

Who Moved My Cheese? An Amazing Way to Deal with Change in Your Work and in Your Life
Charming Your Way to the Top: Hollywood's Premier P.R. Executive Shows You How to Get Ahead
John T. Molloy's New Dress for Success

Chapter 5

The Power of Positive Thinking
Compilations of the many "Complete Idiot's" or "for Dummies" guide books
Excuse Me, Your Life Is Waiting: The Astonishing Power of Feelings
Unleash the Warrior Within: Develop the Focus, Discipline, Confidence, and Courage You Need to Achieve Unlimited Goals
The Disease to Please: Curing the People-Pleasing Syndrome
The Complete Idiot's Guide to Hypnosis

Chapter 6

Bullies, Tyrants, and Impossible People: How to Beat Them without Joining Them
How to Spot a Liar: Why People Don't Tell the Truth . . . and How You Can Catch Them
Random Acts of Kindness
Handwriting Analysis

Chapter 7

How to Succeed in Business without Really Trying!
The Traveler's Gift: Seven Decisions That Determine Personal Success

The Real Scoop

The Pursuit of Happiness: Discovering the Pathway to Fulfillment,
Well-Being, and Enduring Personal Joy
Awaken the Giant Within: How to Take Immediate Control of Your
Mental, Emotional, Physical and Financial Destiny!
10 Secrets for Success and Inner Peace
Think Big: A Think Collection
Too Soon Old, Too Late Smart: Thirty True Things You Need to
Know Now
The Book of Questions
Be Your Own Best Friend: How to Achieve Greater Self-Esteem,
Health, and Happiness
Combination of the "Chicken Soup for the Soul" series and the
"for Dummies" books
Compilation of the many "30-day" promise books
Don't Sweat the Small Stuff

Upcoming Titles

The Five People You Meet in Heaven
Any of the Finding Fulfillment books
Trump: Think Like a Billionaire: Everything You Need to Know
about Success, Real Estate, and Life
10 Stupid Things Women Do to Mess Up Their Lives

About the Authors

Martha Bolton is the author of over seventy books of humor, including *Ouch! Wow!* and *Ha!*, the Official Series, *Didn't My Skin Used to Fit? Cooking with Hot Flashes,* and *Growing Your Own Turtleneck and Other Benefits of Aging.* She was a staff writer for Bob Hope for over fifteen years and has been nominated for an Emmy and a Dove Award. She is the recipient of four Angel Awards. She has also written for Phyllis Diller, Wayne Newton's USO shows, and numerous others. She writes the popular Cafeteria Lady column for *Brio* magazine.

Brad Dickson was a monologue staff writer for *The Tonight Show* with Jay Leno for fourteen years. Prior to that he was a working screenwriter, placing several screenplays with motion-picture companies. Since leaving *The Tonight Show* in January, he has been writing recurring humor columns for the *Los Angeles Times*, *L.A. Daily News* and the Jewish World Review Web site. He's also developing a groundbreaking pilot for a major television network.